DETERMINANTS OF WORLD POLITICS

DETERMINANTS OF WORLD POLITICS

Edited by

PURAN CHANDRA

AKANSHKA PUBLISHING HOUSE
NEW DELHI - 110 059 (INDIA)

AKANSHA PUBLISHING HOUSE
R-37B, Vani Vihar, Uttam Nagar
New Delhi - 110 059
Phones: 25640621, 9811582579
E-mail: ektabooks@yahoo.com

Determinants of World Politics

First Edition 2004

ISBN 81-87606-44-4

PRINTED IN INDIA

Published by M.P. Mishra for Akansha Publishing House, New Delhi - 110 059 and Printed at Tarun Offset Press, Delhi.

Contents

Preface

'World politics' variously known as 'international politics', and 'international relations' etc. is supposed to be regulated by set determinants of political theories. The determining factors are variable.

This book designed as an introductory guide to a subject. Its aim is to discover and point out the basic principles that determine the course of the political relations among sovereign nation-states, and to seek to demonstrate their applicability.

Amdist recent developments in the field of world politics is 'terrorism'. In the name of suppressing terrorism power is polarising time and again and various power nexuses are emerging. Apparently, with the collapse of Soviet Union, World politics has become unipolar revolving around the USA. Recent Iraq War has shown America's ambitions and nefarious designs to dominate the world proving itself the sole super power. Consequently, it seems, there is emerging an anti-American sense among the mulsim countries though clandestinely. Under such circumstances, 'World Politics' will be in shackles and rambles.

This is not a history of recent diplomacy but a real effort to preserve some of the 'scholarly objectivity' that is so frequently a casualty in discussions of contemporary international relations. Primarily prepared for readers, this book will serve as a college text, and it is hoped that the general reader will discover some value in it.

We do not claim to originality as all the things have been told/retold by many authorities one time and again. We have simply the put material in a particular shape. We are grateful to all leading political scientists and philosophers whose theories are cited and reproduced.

Finally Mr. M.P. Misra deserve all appreciation for publishing the book promptly in nice getup.

—Editor

1

Significance of Political Culture

Political culture is the first and foremost determinant of wolrd politics. In every civic society the human nature express itself in matters of values, norms, beliefs, sentiments and attitudes. Human values are transmitted from one generation to another as such or with modifications. This is called, general culture of the society. Some particular aspects of this general culture is essentially concerned with politics related matters. This is called the political culture of that particular society. As such political culture consists of the *emotional and attitudinal environment* within which the *political system operates.* Every political system is based on certain value premises, and is also based on certain goals and ideals. The functioning of a political system is to be judged with reference to a nation's political culture because the citizen's attitude to the political system clearly affects the kind of demands made, the way they are expressed and organized, the reaction of the political system, the nature of popular support etc. thus political culture helps in a significant way in determining the styles of functioning of the political system and also evaluating the same on that basis.

Definitions

Beer and Ulam defines political culture as, "certain aspects of the general culture of the society are especially concerned with how government ought to be conducted and what it shall try to do. This sector of culture, we call political culture."

"Political culture", to Almond and Powell, "is the pattern of individual attitudes and orientations towards politics among the members of a political system".

A.R. Ball says the "political culture is composed of the attitudes, beliefs, emotions and values of a society that relates to the political system and political issues."

Lucian Pye declares political culture as "the set of attitudes, beliefs and sentiments which given order and meaning to the political process and which provide the underlaying assumptions and rules which govern the political behaviour in the political system."

Political culture denotes the attitudes, orientations, sentiments and beliefs of the individuals towards the political objects which prompt him to behave in the political sphere in one way and not in other. But the orientation of the people towards their political object may vary from political system to another. As such the political culture, as witnessed, differs from state to state. While China have a communist culture, USA, UK have essentially democratic culture. Since political culture deals with the attitudes, behaviours, views and perceptions—the changing variables, so it is obvious that political culture is liable to change. Hence political culture lacks consistency and internal cohesion. Political culture is an integral part of the general culture of the society and it is to be studied in the context of the general cultural patterns of the society. Both of them are interlinked with each other and can influence each other in a more or less, legitimate way.

Within a political system, different groups of people may have different orientations towards the political object. These different group orientations which may or may not give rise to an integrated and coherent culture, and clearly distinguishable from one another, are called the subcultures. For example, the tribal culture is the sub culture of the national political culture. Political sub cultures may grow on the basis of region, religion, social class, clan, caste, language, generation, occupation and the like. These sub cultures play a significant role in the process of nation building. In some nations, it is impossible to understand the nature and the character of the national political culture without having a thorough knowledge about its subcultures and their styles of functioning. In India, the subcultural differences on the basis of language, religion, and caste have immense relevance to the working of political system. The existence of such political subcultures may have its positive and negative consequences. In the positive aspect, the existence of a variety of subcultures help in a significant way to understand better the national political culture and its process. But judging from a negative aspect, the existence of such a wide range of political subcultures may kill the consensus in the political system. It may also cause a harm to the common national identity. As such it has a vital impact on the range of conflicts and the complexity of those conflicts between the national political culture and the various subcultures.

It is said that usually a subculture does not question the major structural arrangements of a society, but differs only on certain specific issues related to authoritative decisions. This naturally makes no serious problem for the operators of the political system who can make necessary readjustments by means of value reallocation. But when a political subculture challenges the basic structural arrangements of a society, the stability of the political system is threatened which impels the political authority to use force for quailing the situation. This obviously generates serious tension within the political system. There are three alternatives for the coexistence of subcultures with the national political culture—Process of isolation; Process of assimilation; and Process of accommodation.

Political System: Orientations and Objects

The political culture of a political system denotes to the individual orientations towards the political object which prompts him to behave in a particular way. The functioning of the political system is always by these orientations. To Talcott Parsons, we can divide these orientations into three parts which are the cognitive, affective and evaluative orientation. *Cognitive orientation* refers to the knowledge and awareness that people have towards the political object. *Affective orientation*, is the emotional disposition to the political object thereof. It refers to the feeling of the individual about the political objects–the feeling, either of attachment and involvement or of rejection of that political object. While the *evaluative orientation* refers to the individual perception about the political object and their judgement, essentially rational, on the object by involving the use of values, information and feelings.

These orientations are directed not only towards the formal government institutions such as executive, legislature and judiciary but also towards various political groups such as political parties and pressure groups. It is also directed towards the individual's view of himself as a political actor and also his view of other citizens. Thus the objects towards which the cognitive, affective an evaluative orientation are directed are of four–the political system as a whole, the input process, the output process and the political self.

First object towards which people creates their orientations–cognitive, affective and evaluative, is the political system itself. People have knowledge of, feeling about and judgement on the political system and it is these orientations that condition the development of national identity. To develop these orientations, people must not only be physically and legally the members of the political system but also be psychologically members of that system. Another object of orientation formation is the input process of the political system through which the demands made by the society flows into the political system for their conversion into authoritative policies by means of political action. Thus input objects include the political parties, pressure group and the media of mass communication. The third object towards which the individuals have to form orientation is the output process. It involves the work of bureaucracy, courts and other political institutions which are concerned with the application and implementation of the authoritative decisions. The fourth object of orientation is the concept of political self. As an individual plays a role in the political system as a political actor, he certainly has a knowledge of, attachment to and also his own evaluation of these roles. These subjective orientation to politics they emphasize on the psychological dimension of politics and political culture, so viewed, is an aggregate or patterning of individual 'state of mind'.

Nature and extent of these orientation differs in their magnitude and intensity from nation to nation. As such differs the political culture differs.

Dimensions of Political Culture

The political culture, being essentially the individualistic orientation towards the political objects, have a wide dimension. The input and outputs constitutes the process of the political system. Thus the culture based on that process may be termed as the process culture. Besides the process culture, the political orientation is also directed towards the political system. Although the political culture differs from one political system to another, the dimension of systems culture remains the same. Besides these two–system and process of the government, the individual's role in formation of orientation also extends to the policies of the political system. Thus it may be concluded that there are three broad dimensions of a political culture basing upon the three types of orientations towards the objects. These are–the system culture, the process culture and the policy culture of a political system.

(1) Systems Culture

The first dimension of political culture is related with the political system as a whole. It implies that the orientation of people is directed towards the political system itself. They have their cognitive, affective and evaluative orientation to the governmental institution. The people show their involvement, support and allegiance to the authority based on legitimacy. To quote Max Weber's concept of three types of authority based on three types of legitimacy, the systems culture of a society can also be of three types such as the traditional, the rational legal and the charismatic.

In traditional culture, the people's orientation—cognitive, affective and evaluative, are directed to the traditional authority.

Here faith and obligation to the authority is a matter of personal loyalty to the long established traditions, usages and customs which are usually inherited from the father and forefathers by ascriptive quality.

In rational legal culture, the general orientation of the people is directed not to the individuals holding office, but to the legally established orders which define the status of the person issuing command. Here loyalty is based on impersonal outlook. It is achieved through competition.

In a charismatic culture, the cognitive, affective and evaluative orientation of the people is directed solely to the individual holding public office by virtue of personal trust in him and in his heroism. Here the belief of the people lies on the foundation that the leader or authority who commands possesses some exceptional personal qualities. Such a culture develops when the authority promises to provide a new better future to sway the support of the people. Here the people, being swayed by his promise votes him to power and give him their in alienable support and obedience. The allegiance lasts till the person, holding office dies.

(2) Policy Culture

The policy culture individual's orientation, sentiments, beliefs, values, ethos, emotions and the like are directed not to the system as a whole, but to the policy of the political system. The policy includes not only the inputs but also the output objects. Thus the individual orientation is formed not only to the input structures like political parties, pressure groups and media of mass communication, but also to the output structures consisting of the bureaucracy, courts and other political institutions concerned with the application and implementation of the value judgments of the decision maker which are authoritative in nature.

In a procedural culture, the members of the political system mostly share certain political beliefs and values on the procedure of the political system. This implies that when the political culture of a society assumes a coherent and a fairly homogeneous shape, it means that the members of the system have arrived at a general consensus—consensus either on procedures or on goals.

In objectivinal culture, the orientation of the people, most radically falls into the category of consensus, is directed towards the goal or objective of the political system. Here the people have a knowledge of, feeling about and evaluation of the objective or goal of the political system only.

Objectivinal culture is of two types such as the elite and the mass culture. The elite culture essentially deals with the orientations, values, beliefs and emotions of the rulers who are in charge of making authoritative decisions. As the elites are very much organized and consists of the intellectuals of the society. Their orientation held by other members of the society i.e. the masses.

In contrast to the elite culture lies the mass culture which deals with the individual orientations of the general masses about the goals of the political system. Normally, the masses are influenced by the elites. Thus they automatically subscribe to those goals which are set for them by the elites. The more congruence between the elite and mass culture, the more stable will be the political system itself.

Within a political system, both elite and mass culture intractions gives rise to a set of a particular kind of subculture which Almond and Verba termed as the "role Culture". In more complex political systems there are various specialized structures like bureaucracy, military, political executive, political party, pressure group, interest groups and the media of mass communication etc. which perform certain specific roles. These different specialized roles may represent different political subcultures, given the political system a heterogeneous character. As such the political culture will also be heterogeneous in nature. This heterogeneity, in fact, results from two sources. In the first place, the elites who perform these roles may be recruited from the particular political subculture. And secondly, the process of their induction and socialization into these roles may give rise to different values, loyalties and cognitive orientations. Since these elites play a vital role in the political process, the kind of cultural differences they represent may have a great impact on the performance of the political system.

(3) Process Culture

The third dimension of political culture is the process culture. Here the individual attitudes, orientations, beliefs, sentiments and values, all are directed to the political process only. The individual develops his cognitive, affective and evaluative orientation towards the input process as well as towards the output process. The individuals are concerned with how inputs are fed, output came out and feedback develops etc. hence it is a collective activity.

The process culture has two subcategories such as the view of others and the view of self.

Trust

An important aspect of political culture is a high level of inter-personal trust that facilitates the political cooperation and political involvement. Here the decisions are reached by mutual consensus through consultation and compromise. It does not mean that there is always a unanimous decision. One may oppose some actions of others which he may feel necessary for doing so. It does not mean hostility. But in most of the cases, the decision is taken by unanimous achievements. Here the individuals are engaging themselves in peaceful competition with those of opposing political views. The greater is the amount of interpersonal trust and confidence, the stronger are the ties of horizontal integration of the members of a political system that ensures the stability of the political system by infusing a sense of pride among the people and by enabling them to maintain a high level of civility in their political intercourse.

Hostility

When an individual tries to oppose each and every policy of the government in the out group, they develop hostile attitude towards other individuals exercising political actions. Thus there is no question of compromise, no development and no trust worthiness among the people in particular, and in the political system in general. When the hostility culture develops among the people, there is always a kind of fear psychosis exists among them which hampers the process of nation building. For instance, when the British political culture is characterized by a wide spread interpersonal trust, the political cultures of Italy, Mexico, Ethiopia reveals a great amount of distrust and suspicion in social relations.

Parochial Political Culture

When an individual becomes aware of his local system, local issues and involves himself in local politics, ignoring the national political system and national issues, it is called parochial political culture. So it is a narrow culture which reflects the local politices only. Here an individual have no cognition of the political system, and as such, they do not have also any effective and evaluative orientation towards the political system. Beyond his locality, an individual has no involvement in the national input, output, feedback and conversion process. He is parochial in the sense, that for the satisfaction of his wants, he looks only to his family, or to the community or perhaps depends on his own efforts.

Such a type of political culture is rarely found to be in modern industrial societies; its ideal place of setting is in the traditional society where there are no specialized roles, and people were unaware of the national political system.

Subject Culture

The subject political culture is one in which there is high frequency of orientation to the political system as a whole and also to the output process; but where the cognitive, affective and evaluative orientations to the input structures and also towards the self as a political actor, is extremely low. Here the individual's position is essentially, a passive one. One sees no possibility of influencing the system, and silently by accepting the decisions as authoritative and unchallengeable tries to take benefit out of its implementation. One interprets role as one in which one must accept the system as it is, not try to change it. This type of political culture is most prominent in East European countries and also in many newly independent nations of Asia and Africa.

Participant Culture

In a participant political culture, the individual, on the other hand, is seen and sees himself as an active participant in the political process. Here his cognitive, affective and evaluative orientations – all are very high with regard to the political system as a whole, to the inputs, outputs, feedback and conversion process as well as to the self as a political actor. Here people participate in making demands, policies, getting the benefits and evaluating them. It is also termed as the rationally- activist political culture because the individual is both rational and active in nature.

These three types of political cultures are, however, only the utopian types; none of them can be found in its pure form in any society since all the individuals with in a political system cannot be expected to the oriented in the same way and to the same extent. Accordingly, Almond and Verba lists out the following mixed types of political cultures:

(i) Parochial – subject

(ii) Subject – participant

(iii) Parochial-participant and

(iv) The civic political culture.

In *parochial-subject political culture*, the individual has knowledge about a variety of governmental roles although he is mostly unaware of the ways in which he can influence the political system. In this cultural system, the sense of self as a political force is very much vague and undeveloped and the input structures of the society are poorly defined.

The *subject-participant* type is represented by a society where some of the citizens are very much politically aware and also active and the rest are relatively passive. The former are naturally found to develop positive orientations to all types of political objects. Here the average citizens know that he must be active and be a participant, but is given, in fact, very little opportunity for sharing in the decisions.

In *Parochial-participant* type of political culture, the input institutions are relatively local like tribal and caste associations although the national output institutions are quite well developed. But in any case, both the inputs and outputs institutions are so much under the pressure of parochial interests that their performance as national participatory organs in greatly affected.

The civic political culture is an analysis of the details of political culture of British, United States, Germany, Italy and Mexico. Judging from the individual's cognitive and emotional attitude towards the system, his relation with the input and output structures and the individual's conception about his own capabilities and role, the civic culture is an ideal culture which combines the characteristics of three ideal type of political culture–parochial, subject and participant. It represents a synthesis of directive and acquiescent, participant and passive attitudes. Here the subject orientations and participant orientations are equally strong. While the former allows the elites to function with sufficient initiative and freedom, the latter force those elites to remain subject to popular preferences.

As Almond and Verba describes civic cultures contains parts of the 'rationality–activist' culture. It is a more mixed political culture. Here political activity, rationality and involvement are balanced by passivity, traditionality and political indifference. The citizen is neither so deeply involved and active in politics as to destroy the ability of the government to make authoritative decisions nor so inactive and indifferent as to give the political elites complete freedom in decision making. This more balanced civic culture is based upon a more general set of non-political-social norms and attitudes-norms of interpersonal trust and cooperation that penetrate the political system. This culture develops both the essence of potential personal competence and the essence of trusting other people. The sense of competence and trust allow the citizens to feel at each with government; and in that, he will not feel it necessary to oppose the government on all issues but does feel competent to associate in opposing it on all issues he feels to be important. Similarly the norms of participation allows the government to act freely and fairly but it is also a constraint on the government abusing its freedom to act.

The citizens, in a civic culture, has a "reserve of influence". He is a potentially active citizen whose interest in political life is not necessarily high but whose general role of extra-political activity is essentially high.

Thus the civic political culture is one where the citizens and the political system maintain a correct relationship with each other, where the democratic citizen is active, yet passive, involved, yet not too much involved; influential, yet differential; where the citizens do not overload the political system with all sorts of demands but they are processed and channellized through interest groups; where the various segment of people maintain a cross-cutting relationship with each other whose demands and aspirations are integrated through the political parties; in short, where the political culture a homogeneous shape and character.

According to Almond and Verba, "The culture prevalent in Anglo-American countries, thus, is a pluralistic culture based on persuation and communication, a culture of consensus and diversity, a culture that permitted change but moderated it. . . ."

Role and Utility of Political Culture

Within a political system, the role of political culture is diverse in nature. This characterizes the dynamic view of political culture. The values and attitudes which constitutes the part of a political culture are sought to be diffused among the members of the society through the mechanism of political socialization. The idea of political culture represents an effort to study the total political system without disregarding the peculiarities of individual psychology. In this way political culture attempts at a synthesis between psychology and sociology and thus reaps the benefits of both micro analysis and macro analysis.

Political culture serves as a framework for perception and evaluation of society as a whole or of the political system. Through it, we can perceive the institutions, the society, the system's performance etc. Thus it is an optical lens through which an individual can see the system and evaluate its functioning.

It also acts as a set of guide line principles for political action. The individual's orientation towards the objects are formed which prompts him to act in a way judged by himself. Thus political culture helps in making the individuals active and participant in the political process of the society.

Political culture is psychological in nature. A political culture functions as a legitimization instrument. The system is based on authority; authority on legitimacy and legitimacy is based on culture. So political culture, as an legitimization instrument, influence the general political system of the country. However, while legitimacy is a legal phenomena.

Political culture relates to larger issues of political development and as such it acts as an instrument for bridging the gap between governmental decisions and people's participation. The study of political culture through individual interviews and responses and case studies of individual actions on the one hand, and by means of aggregate statistics and group behaviour pattern studies, on the other hand, we could systematically apprehend the totality of individual orientations that conditions the performance of the political system.

The significance of the study of political culture lies in the fact that by means of it, we may know whether the members of a political system have been able to arrive at a consensus that ensures the stability of the system. When the political culture achieves a coherent character, if implies that consensus have already achieved. The growth of consensus is intimately connected with the question about the degree of congruence between the political structures and political culture.

When a society reaches an optimum level of congruence between its political structures and political culture, it is too far unrealistic to expect that the political system will have a single uniform political culture. In fact, every society reveals a fundamental difference between the culture of the rulers and that of the masses. The higher is the congruence between these two cultures i.e. the elite culture and mass cultures, the greater is the homogeneity of the political culture that ensures the stability of the political system.

The relationship between the elite culture and mass culture is of crucial importance in a democratic system. Since democracy essentially thrives on consensus, it cannot of course, flourish in an atmosphere of antagonism between the elite culture and mass culture. In democracy, the elites usually try to combat this problem by subjecting themselves along with the non elites to a democratic myth that ordinary citizens ought to participate in politics and that they are, in fact, influential, here thus the elite do not really dwarf their powers in favour of the masses but they punctuate their powers with a sense of responsiveness. Thus a fairly high degree of homogeneity is established between the elite culture and the mass culture in a democratic political system. Thus political culture widens the prospects of democracy.

Another prospect of political culture is that it helps in the process of nation building. It facilitates nation building through a high level of interpersonal trust and confidence that facilitates political cooperation and political involvement without which democratic politics is not possible.

An equally important aspect of political culture is that it strengthen the public opinion in the society. This can be facilitated through the people's subjective sense of political competence. This sense of political competence is measurable to the extent to which a citizen feels that he can influence and participate in the decision making process. This subjective competence, however, is not actual political competence.

The political culture helps in achieving unity in diversity. Within a political system various sub-cultural groups may exist which have developed their own cultural traits. In spite of the existence of several sub-cultural groups, the congruence is achieved in the political system through the development of a systematic congruent national political culture. In the development of such congruent political culture, symbols often play an important role. National flag, national song, national anthem, old institutions like monarchy in Britain, political rituals like ceremonial opening of parliament, religious rituals like coronation ceremonies as in Britain—these and many other symbols are constantly made use of to evoke people's emotional attachment to the reverence for the political system.

Being dynamic, a political culture changes as a result of its result of its response to new ideas, industrialization, the impact of new leaders, population changes and many other factors. Incorporating these changes, it continues from generation to generation through the process of political socialization.

Any society which is class divided must ultimately be controlled by those political values and ideals which favour the ruling class. Sometimes, the interests of different class may temporarily coincide and generate certain values and ideas which may be truly representative in character. Gunnar Myrdal opines, "India is ruled by a selected group of upper class citizens who use their political power to secure their privileged position." The economic and political power in India essentially belongs to the proprieted classes who have continued to monopolize education and mass culture. The gap between rich and poor is being perpetuated and intensified by the operation of power mechanism. A study of political culture, however, is incomplete without proper understanding of the process of political socialization.

The foregoing discussion makes it obvious that the 'political culture' is a significant determinant of world politics.

2

Introduction to Nation-State

What is the State?

The state is a politically organized body of people occupying a definite territory, living under a government, and incorporating sovereignty. This definition is sufficiently broad to encompass all the states involved in international politics despite the almost infinite variety in details which exists among them. In the language of international politics, the word 'state' usually be read 'government'.

The government is the portion of the state that actually conducts foreign affairs, exercising the collective power and making decisions in the name of the whole. 'International' and 'Inter-state' relations are, thus, actually inter-governmental' relations. The state is central to world politics. Individuals, of course, play a critical role; the state can function in the real world only by means of the action of human beings. Individuals gain significance in international affairs, however, only when they become clothed with corporate authority arising from an official connection with a state.

This applies whether the person involved is Prime Minister Khaleda Zia or John Doe, a conscript in his national army. Neither is important as a person, but rather because of official role.

Statehood: Common Characteristics

All states, regardless of their differences in terms of other criteria, have four characteristics in common: people, territory, government, and sovereignty. Certain aspects of each of these should be considered in some detail.

People

The number of people necessary to statehood may be widely different from one state to another. Are there any limits upon the size of a population? More specifically, is there are maximum or minimum figure beyond which the size of a population impairs statehood?

Minimum Population. In theoretical sense, the absolute minimum population of a state for international purposes would appear to be one, provided that that one person were accepted and recognized by other states and that they were capable of discharging the responsibilities of statehood. As a practical matter, however, all that can be said is that a state must have sufficient population to enable it to accomplish its international mission. Although this resembles the ancient law to the effect that a man's legs should be long enough to reach the ground, it does reflect the actual situation. The minimum size of a population is a relative factor rather than an absolute number. Luxembourg, for example, has been able to maintain its international identity despite a tiny population, while large concentrations of people throughout Asia and Africa proved unable to avoid colonialism.

Maximum Population. The eighteenth-century French philosopher, Charles de Second at, Baron de Montesquieu, maintained that it was possible for a state to grow too populous. His argument, which gained widespread acceptance for a time, was that after a certain point was passed in population growth, efficient government would prove impossible and the state would split. The point has considerable validity for the time; history affords many examples of states, such as the Roman Empire, that suffered dissolution as a partial result of over-expansion. Today, however, the problem of maintaining control over large concentrations of people has been largely solved. It would be technically feasible to organize the entire world under a single government if modern devices of transportation and communication were given their maximum geographic effect.

While it remains true that in certain 'backward' areas of the world (such as China) an over large population impairs efficient government, no general rule can be deduced from these instances, indeed, there seems to be no logical upper limit to the possible population of a state. Maximum population, like minimum population, is relative to circumstances.

Territory

No generalization can be laid about the minimum territory necessary to statehood except to point out that it must be extensive enough to provide a base for mounting power sufficient to achieve its objectives. Obviously, question of territory interact upon those population; a great but sparsely populated territory can acquire statehood only with much more difficulty than a smaller but more thickly settled area.

Maximum Territory. Maximums of territory (like those of population) are not arrived at by establishing any raw figure, but instead are considered as functions of the level of technological development of the particular state. Today states of continental expanse leaders in world affairs, and their great size—far from being a source of weakness—contributes to their strength. On the other hand smaller but less well-organized states, such as Burma and Indonesia, have great difficulty in exercising effective control over their outlying regions.

State without Territory. The question of the continued existence of a state after it has lost all its territory has arisen during both great wars of this century. It has been most pressing in the case of the various governments-in-exile forced to flee from hostile armies, such as the governments of Poland and Czechoslovakia during World War II, and the Tibet later on. Their dominion over territory was suspended by conquest, but they retained their identity and were able to exercise control over émigr population and financial resources. The officials view of the western allied in both wars was that the government's continued to represent actual states.

This position agrees with the legal theory of statehood as well as the practical requirements of world politics. It would seem, however, that although state existence may continue temporarily without any territory during a period when state authority is in suspension, it cannot be argued that it can, thus, continue permanently or indefinitely.

Government

Government consists of the public institutions for the accomplishment of state purposes. Every state must have a government, although within broad limits each state may erect such particular structures as it desires.

International Requirements. International life imposes a few requirements which must be met by any government. Effective arrangements must exist for the conduct of international relations. This pattern of offices must be competent to conduct diplomacy, to commit the state to action, and to take such action.

The techniques of international intercourse stabilized in the days of absolute monarchs. It was, therefore, long ago established that there must be a determine human head of government in every state. This person alone may officially speak for the state, and he is legally responsible for all policy steps taken by his government.

This principle is in full effect today. The President of the United States, the Prime Minister of Great Britain, and the Premier (president du conseil) of France, all occupy such positions. Foreign states have official contacts only with this official, his principal deputy for foreign affairs (ordinarily the foreign minister or corresponding official), and with other designated subordinates. With the remainder of the governmental organization they have little concern.

A further requirement of a government is that it be capable of accepting responsibility for its decision and actions. Treaties, once made, must be observed; policy decisions must be executed. It would serve little purposes for a government to make solemn promises and then, to be too weak or too divided to carry out them.

The maintenance of international responsibility means,

therefore, that the government which speaks for the state must actually be exercising effective control over its population and territory. Inability to do this usually deprives the state to its full international role.

Domestic Freedom of Action. After satisfying these few requirements, states may organize their governments very differently. Some have elaborate mechanisms for registering and executing popular will, while others confine the decision-making power to a small elite. The government may be strong or it may be weak; it may be stable or unstable; the people may be happy, quiescent, or restive and potentially revolutionary. All this is in the strictest sense irrelevant to international relations.

With any question of 'good' and 'bad' government no other state has any legal right to deal if the state is organized to fulfil its international responsibilities the arrangement of its international political functions is its own affair.

The functioning of the government of a state becomes a matter of international concern only in exceptional circumstances. If internal political convulsions impair or destroy the capacity of the state to play its international part, other states may legitimately take note of this fact. If the state is unable to exercise its sovereignty in international relations, other states may suspend intercourse with the incompetent state, and resume official relations when stability has been restored and the international personality of the state is again complete.

This was the course followed by most states at the time of the Bolshevik revolution in Russia in 1917. The collapse of the Czarist government eventuated in the rupture of normal international contacts with the new Russian government.

Full relations were entered into again after several years as, one at a time, the other states of the world satisfied themselves that the Soviet government was capable of accepting international responsibility, at least upon a minimum basis. In the same way for the same alleged reasons, the United States had persisted in its refusal to extend recognition to the Communist government of China since 1949.

Sovereignty

Internal Sovereignty. Sovereignty has sometimes been referred to as 'the supreme political characteristic'. Although definitions abound, the general import of the term is clear. There must be, in order for a society to become and remain in state, a law-making authority in the state beyond which there is no legal appeal. When thought of as the source of domestic law—usually termed 'internal' sovereignty—the concept is comprehensible.

It would be difficult to preserve even minimum order and peace within a society without there being some final source of law; the conduct of more elaborate governmental functions would be impossible.

As long as voluntary cooperation cannot be counted upon to produce the social results men demand of government today, the state must continue to be the processor of final legal authority.

External Sovereignty. The World politics, however, is especially concerned with a different aspect of sovereignty. If it is true that in each state there is a legal authority that recognizes no superior, what will be the basis of the relationships between any two such states?

Sovereignty has an international as well as domestic implication. Sovereignty means the legal freedom of the state from external control. Unless a state is free to determine its own national interest, lay down its own policy objectives, and to devise techniques for their attainment completely in terms of its own desires and without dictation from any foreign state, it cannot be considered as sovereign.

International law also recognizes many 'semi-sovereign' political organizations. Some governments possess internal sovereignty but have lost (or never acquired) the power and the right to conduct independent foreign policies. An example of a small unit of this type is the Principality of Monaco; larger ones include the governments of Nepal and Bhutan in Central Asia.

A second classification of 'semi-sovereignties' includes such international oddities as the 'Free City' of Danzig between 1919 and 1939 and the 'Free Territory' of Trieste between 1945 and 1954. The former was created under the sponsorship of the League of Nations, the latter, by the United Nations. Both enjoyed only a short period of existence, ultimately being absorbed into their larger neighbours.

Another border line group is formed by the many small states today that are so completely under the domination of a larger and more powerful ally as to raise serious doubts about their sovereign status.

Was Bulgaria or Poland sovereign in any real international sense, or is Panama? Although the legal niceties were observed and these 'satellites' possess all the visible signs of sovereign statehood, no one, for a moment, believed that the major elements of their foreign policies are independently determined.

Sovereign and the United Nations. Are all the members of the United Nations sovereign states? Article II of the Charter of the United Nations stipulates that the organization is founded upon the principle of the 'sovereign equality' of all its members, and practice and interpretation of the Charter agree that membership is available only to sovereign states.

The State: Legal Nature

International law considers the state to be the 'international person'. The only entities recognized in international practice as full participants are the states themselves; individual human beings have no international status except as we noted above. International politics therefore, goes on among states as corporate beings; this legal assumption invests the state with certain juristic characteristics.

The State as Corporation

We can understand the legal nature of the state in easy manner by making a comparison with an institution with which most Indians have some familiarity, the private corporation. This approach throws much light upon some of the peculiarities of state existence.

The Analogy with the Corporation. The state, like the corporation, is held to be a person before the law in its external sense; both state and corporation, however, are abstract beings whose only existence is a legal one. A corporation may own property; a state may acquire territory (real property) and wealth (personal property).

A corporation makes contracts; a state enters into treaties (many of the provisions of ordinary contract law apply to the law of treaties as well). A corporation may sue and be sued; a state may also become subject to formal jurisprudence, before an international court.

The obligations of a state, like those of corporation, continue independently of whatever particular persons are holding office within the government. Transformation of regimes has no legal effect. The revolutionary government of France in 1791, for example, succeeded to all the legal advantages and disabilities of the monarchical government it has replaced. In the same way, the Bolshevik government of Russia was unable to gain international consent to its proposal to repudiate the international debts contracted by the Czars. No principle of international law is more firmly grounded in practice that this rule of 'state succession'; in its essentials it is the identical doctrine that governs the practice of corporations.

Internal Independence of the State. As already noted that states have no legal right to concern themselves with the internal affairs of their fellows. This principle grows out of the idea of the corporate personality of the state. The legal facade of 'statehood' is a barrier beyond which no external agency may rightfully go.

Whether or not the people of a state are efficiently governed, happy, or free is an 'internal' question, and the monolithic 'unity' of the state does not permit any legitimate grounds for questioning from the outside. Just as the motives of an individual are usually not open to legal question so long as his behaviour is within the law, so also are the purely internal affairs of a state free from international scrutiny.

Many attempts have been made in recent years to force certain ruling groups to accept international responsibility for internal policies, but no marked change in the general rule has resulted. Nazi treatment of the Jews in Germany was condemned by civilized people everywhere, but it required the catastrophe of the Second World War to bring that policy to an end.

The United Nations had sought to force the government of the Union of South Africa to modify its restrictive policy toward its non-white population, but the doctrine of internal sovereignty had stood firm against pressure, even from a world organization. Too many states are jealous of their own independence to be interested in setting a precedent that might some day be turned against them.

Legal Immunity of Officials. Similar as in the case of the corporation, government officials enjoy personal immunity from responsibility for official acts. Although the state, as an abstract being, is powerless to act by itself and all its functions are carried out by human agents, these individuals are not legally liable to any external agency.

Their responsibility is internal; international law is powerless to touch them. Penalties may be imposed upon the state, but its officials are protected by a cloak of legal anonymity. An analogous rule is found in corporation law; the principal in a transaction is responsible for the acts of his agent.

The 'war crimes' trials after World War II were hailed as modification in this principle and as establishing a rule of private responsibility under international law. Many 'war criminals' in Germany and Japan were tried for their parts in the unsuccessful aggressions undertaken by their governments. Although penalties ranging from death to imprisonment were imposed upon many of the accused by special international tribunals, the broader implications of the verdicts have not been widely accepted as expressing a settled legal rule.

Many critics argue the idea of personal responsibility would be destructive of governmental efficiency and provocative of disobedience and evasion among government personnel. As a result many governments, including that of the United States, have found the principle unpalatable.

Now the war crimes verdicts are generally thought of as examples of 'victor's justice' and the notion of the immunity of government officials is not seriously challenged in world affairs.

Legal Consequences of Statehood

As is seen that legally the state is a personality and that the international order is composed of such self-contained entities engaged in relations with one another. Certain consequences arise logically from the general concept.

Equality. The first of these is the equality of states. If all states are complete legal sovereigns and none recognizes a common superior, perfect equality among them is the only possible basis of interstate relations. This legal principle obviously does violence to the political facts. States, in any rational political sense, are not at all equal; we have seen that inequality is normal by almost any criterion. Nevertheless, equality before the law is the theoretical basis of much of the day-by-day conduct of international affairs.

Formal international intercourse—diplomacy—proceeds upon the assumption of the equal status of all states. Treaties—even punitive treaties dictated by a victorious state to a vanquished enemy—are deemed to be agreements between legal equals.

Much protocol is devoted to the demonstration and attempted proof of this idea. One of the continuing tasks of a diplomat is to arrange affairs so that the political factors that actually determine the course of events do not to do irreparable injury to the fiction of state equality. It is important to preserve the illusion of equality status because, like so many other legal fictions, it has considerable practical utility; for example, it provides the only possible base for international legal action.

Independence. Very closely allied with the idea of equality is the principle of the independence of states. As sovereignties, they may be bound only by their own consent and then only for so long as they wish to remain so. This is obviously another legal fiction; politically, states have only as much real independence of action as they have power to enforce or that they are permitted to exercise by the tacit consent of stronger states. Yet, so appealing is the idea of freedom that many statesmen go to great lengths to make clear that their course of action is their own choice and not dictated from outside.

Seldom a state will reject an otherwise desirable policy for no more rational reason that its insistence upon avoiding the appearance of external dictation. What the legal doctrine of independence tends to mean in practice is state irresponsibility. If a state is legally free to select any policy objectives it wishes and to implement them by whatever means are expedient, and if it can do this without reference to any set of fixed principles or to any international body, it is obviously behaving irresponsibility.

A state may ultimately suffer the legal consequences of its action, but this is uncertain at best; furthermore, no legal means exists to prevent it from anti-social action. No form of international 'preventive jurisprudence' exists, for states are legally free agents.

Jurisdiction. A legal consequences of statehood with more real content than the proceeding two is its jurisdiction over territory and people. A state exercises authority and power over all the territory within its boundaries and over all people residing therein.

There are some relatively minor exceptions to this rule, but it is applicable in most instances. The state also retains jurisdiction over its nationals when they are outside its territory. The legal power gives a broader sanction to political authority than mere physical force and is generally regarded as absolute. Conflicts of jurisdiction between states are not uncommon. Sometimes they arise out of overlapping claims of territory, sometimes out of dual authority over particular individuals or pieces of property. National citizenship laws, for example, overlap to such an extent that it is not unusual for a person to have citizenship in two states simultaneously.

For example, under current statutes, an American woman who carries a Norwegian citizen retains her American citizenship by United States law but gains Norwegian citizenship as the wife of a citizen under the laws of Norway. Although such jurisdiction conflicts are usually sustained without great difficulty, it is not a happy condition in which to be found if the lawful commands of the two governments conflict.

Responsibility. As an outgrowth of the power of jurisdiction, states must also assume legal responsibility for events which occur on their territory or as a result of actions by their nationals while abroad. The responsibility is corporate, not individual; remedial action is taken by the government in the name of the state.

The principle of state responsibility works in reverse also. Not only does a state accept liability when one of its citizens errs; it also protects and assists him when his rights are invaded when he is abroad.

'State' in World Politics

We may gain an entirely different view of the state if we shift our emphasis from its legal characteristics and consider it as a 'political organization'—as a participant in international politics. From this point of view the state and its government may be thought of as the structure of public institutions through which a social group works in order to achieve its political objectives.

In other words, the state is a group of people organized for the accomplishment of common political purposes. The government is the active arm of the state. Human beings and government, therefore, are the political components of the state.

Functions of the State

(1) *Community Mission*. In all modern states, the people look to government to aid them in reaching certain goals, both

private and public. This is true both in internal affairs and in international relations. Individuals, organized under government into a state, are able to mobilize political power that the government may use in the common interest.

The objectives of the state are largely imposed upon it by popular demand. In a political sense, international politics is the struggle between organized social groups, with governments serving as the media of contact, for the accomplishment of those objectives which each group feels to be necessary or desirable.

(2) *Internal Functions*. The functions that people demand of the state are usually divided into the categories of 'internal' and 'external' (or 'domestic' and 'foreign'), although it is not possible to draw a clear line between them.

Internally, the state is initially charged with the task of protection. In every society, government has the duty of protecting the individual against other individuals, against society, and against himself, in other words, the government must maintain public order and redress individual grievances. The state everywhere also has a welfare function. Although each political group works out to its own satisfaction the field of its welfare activity and the extent to which the government is to go in improving the lot of the individuals, it is pretty well agreed throughout the civilized world that the state has a responsibility to guarantee and to improve in some way the happiness and well-being of its citizens.

In recent past the trend has been toward the radical expansion of this welfare activity; today, at least in the western world, the older protective and regulatory activity of the state is largely overshadowed.

(3) *External Functions*. The external functions of the state do not permit of being so neatly catalogued. We shall see later that the state mechanism serves the national interest in international politics and that each people's version of national interest is determined by factors peculiar to themselves. It is not inaccurate to say, however, that the foreign policies of most states have two aspects, not dissimilar to the dual internal function

of government. Protection and welfare appear in external state activity as well as in internal.

The Issue of Sovereignty

'Political behaviourists', armed with the findings of modern sociology and psychology, question the validity of the idea of sovereignty by denying the existence of any institutional power and explaining obedience to law as arising from a combination of consent, coercion, and habit.

'Political pluralists' demonstrate that the state does not, in fact, monopolize law-making power, but that instead it shares it with other groups. Indeed, so general have become the attacks that the whole juristic theory of the state (founded upon the doctrine of sovereignty) is, in general, disrepute in academic circles today. At the international level, these critics claim that sovereignty, if it means anything at all, must include the ideas of the independence and the equality of all states. This condition, they claim, does not exist and never has existed; even if it were possible to realize, it would be undesirable.

Definitely the pure doctrine of sovereignty must be constantly modified by the realistic conditions of international political life; perhaps, the modifications are necessarily so great as to impair the validity and utility of the whole idea.

Persistence of the Doctrine. States, although they may not, in fact, be really sovereign and independent, persist in acting and thinking as if they were. Effective institutional control over their actions is generally lacking and they yield only to the superior power of other states.

National policies incorporate the assumption that a state is ultimately answerable only to itself. This is most unsetting when large states exercise their free choice to plunge the world into war for their own private reasons, but throughout the entire international scene the idea of sovereignty acts to make world politics dynamic and unpredictable.

Sovereignty in terms of national independence is intimately associated with the urges of nationalism, and popular demand often forces statesman today to insist upon the literate letter of the privileges of sovereignty even though such action might result in injury to the state's true interest. India's termination of dominion status in 1949, France's reluctance to permit the rearmament of Germany between 1949 and 1954, and American insistence after 1949 upon an inflexible policy toward Communist China, and all recent examples of this tendency. The doctrine of national sovereignty may be what it is sometimes call—an unrealistic and pernicious fallacy— but it is political fact of which statesmen and students alike must take account.

Nationalism

The significant states of the world today are nation-states; that is, they possess the common characteristics of statehood and in addition the people of each feel themselves united into a nation. The transformation of the state proper into the nation-state has had a profound influence upon international politics; nationalism is today one of the dominant forces in world affairs.

Nature of Nationalism

The Nation. Although the literature of political science provides many attempted definitions of 'nation', there does not exist complete definitions of 'nation', there does not exist complete agreement on its essential components. There is general understanding, however, that a nation is a people's sharing a spirit of unity that makes them to live together under the same government and to see their state prosper.

Many suggestions have been made beyond this generalization, as to the specific unifying factors that wield a people into a nation. A common language, a common religion, a common racial background, or a common cultural heritage are among the most frequently cited of these.

Though most of the nations of the world do possess all or some of these characteristics, it is not possible to claim that they are of universal applicability.

There are nations that do not have a common language,

such as Switzerland; nations of great religious diversity, such as the United States; nations without racial 'purity', such as India; nations without cultural homogeneity, such as Canada.

The most that we can conclude is that nationhood is the product of a mass emotion and that is can arise from any of great variety of stimuli. Those mentioned above are only the most common bases of this emotion.

Nationalism as Mass Emotion. Nationalism is the emotion of nationhood. A nationalistic people feels itself an entity different from the total of state which each citizen is supposed to accept as personally desirable. The nation's friends and enemies become the friends and enemies of each individual; the nation's successes and failures become individual victories and individual defeats.

Most often these reactions arise independently of any personal involvement; Frenchmen, for example, traditionally hate and fear Germany, even though many particular Frenchman have never suffered pain or disability at the hands of any German.

The immediate effect of the spirit of unity of modern nations is to influence the individual to merge his identity with the greater whole of the nation. As a part of the mass, he reacts with it, responds to the same stimuli, performs the same-ritualistic acts. A population sufficiently nationalistic will behave as a unit, crushing dissent and making conformity to the patriotic code of a matter of high civic duty.

Nationalism in International Politics

Nationalism has a long history, but as a preponderant force in international affairs it dates generally from the era of the French Revolution, at the end of the eighteenth century.

The rulers of revolutionary France, beset by enemies on all sides, succeeded in convincing the masses of the French people that each Frenchman had a personal stake in the government's policy. From that day forward, the spirit of nationalism has played an increasingly significant role in the framing of foreign policies.

The Democratization of Foreign Policy. The greatest result of the rise of modern nationalism has been the 'democratization' of foreign policy. A population, since its members are to be called upon to execute government policy by military service (the rise of nationalism made possible the mass conscript army) and, perhaps, to die for it, today demands and receives a voice in its formulation.

No matter how authoritarian the government may be, every statesman keeps in constant touch with the nationalist feelings of his people. The major elements of all foreign policies are in reality determined by the nationalist attitudes of the respective peoples. As new areas of the world have come under the influence of nationalism, rulers in those states have discovered that the direction of foreign affairs is to a large extent taken out of their hands and transferred to popular mass control. The old government elite still makes the detailed decisions and operated the government machinery, but their actions must be confined within the limits laid down by popular opinion.

Recently, Leaders in a number of states in the Middle East and Southeast Asia have on a number of occasions underestimated the power of a newborn nationalism, only to find themselves in serious difficulty as a result. Governments in Egypt, Iran, Burma and Indonesia (among others) have been required since 1949 to make hasty alteration in their policy to make allowance for the new demands of nationalism.

Nationalism as a Tool of Policy. Policy makers find nationalism a convenient tool of policy. Let a policy maker decide that a given step is wise and expedient; all he need do in order to gain the necessary popular support is to identify the policy in question with the nationalist credo. Nationalism makes public duty (including support of the government) a sacred trust of the individual. In the public interest he is expected to be willing to sacrifice his personal liberty, his property, and even his life. With this kind of mass support, any statesman finds his lot much easier. To a leader engaged in a risky or reckless course, it is usually a matter of sheer necessity to be backed by an inflamed an uncompromising public opinion.

To the more conservative statesman, nationalist support

provides a basis upon which to proceed and a protection in the event of unexpected adversity. Failure to identify policy with nationalist goals by either type of policy maker open the government to the danger of popular repudiation.

Rigidity of Nationalism. Statesmen have also discovered, however, that a sensitive nationalism may on occasion prove to be a serious hindrance to the execution of a realistic foreign policy. A strong nationalist spirit tends to be very firm in its likes and dislikes, thus robbing the policy maker of much of his necessary flexibility and freedom of manoeuvre.

Certain states may be objects of nationalist hatred, as in the case of Turkish attitudes toward Russia; certain policy objectives may become sanctified by tradition far beyond their true worth, such as British insistence upon the historic 'lifeline' of the Empire which passes through Gibralter and Suez.

Strong attachments may be formed for certain states or regimes; one pertinent illustration of this attitude is proved by American admiration for Chiang Kai-shek and the Kuomintang government of China.

Less obvious than the foregoing is nationalist identification with certain techniques and procedures of policy.

American Nationalism, for example, distrusts propaganda as a device; British nationalism still yearns for the strategy of the balance of power despite present circumstances that make it unfeasible.

Changing any of these attitudes is most difficult and always at least potentially dangerous. It is easier for statesmen to be guided by them. Nationalism, thus, creates rigid channels along which the policy maker must move in designing strategies; all major policy decisions must obtain formal or informal popular ratification before success, or even maximum efforts, can be achieved.

In today's rapidly moving world, over-rigid nationalist viewpoints frequently conflict with changing conditions. Governments often find themselves in a position to gain great advantage or at least to avoid suffering a setback—if they take rapid action in a crisis situation.

Frequently, however, this action would conflict with the nationalist desires of the people. In such a case, the policy maker has variety of alternatives open to him, all of them more or less unhappy. He may choose to flout public opinion, trusting either that success of his policy will ultimately win popular approval or else, in case of failure, that the resulting popular outcry will die down without causing the repudiation of his policy. He may conduct a hurried programme of 'educating' his people to the necessity of the new step—a move of uncertain value at best. He may temporize, hoping for a turn of events that will make the unpopular decision unnecessary. He may, finally, drift with the currents of opinion, even though he might feel that their direction is wrong and will result either in a lost opportunity for constructive action or else a positive defeat. In any case his lot is made harder by the inflexibility of nationalist stereotypes and the emotional orientation of much public opinion on foreign policy.

An acute instance of the pervasive influence of nationalism is afforded by the course of international politics since 1945. Statesmen, working in an atmosphere of constant crisis and keenly aware of the possibility of global war, have found it dangerously easy to gain popular support for key policy steps by exciting nationalist passions to a high pitch.

Playing upon fears of alien ideologies and the deeply rooted attachment men feel for familiar and sacred beliefs, governments everywhere have stirred their peoples to demand the dangerous moves which the leadership has already decided to be necessary and desirable. To their sorrow, many statesmen have learned that nationalist emotions are easy to call into existence and to intensify, but difficult to control and sometimes impossible to dispel when the reason for their original appearance has disappeared.

Governments have often been pushed beyond the point at which they were aiming by the pressures of public opinion.

Egypt and Iran, among many others, have had cause since 1951 to regret the unleashing of mass nationalism upon a delicate political situation.

Manipulation of Nationalist Symbols. Nationalism, being emotional rather than rational, gains specific content for most people through symbols. These may assume many forms. National flags are among the most common; so are national uniforms and ceremonies such as the changing of the guard Buckingham Palace and the dress parade of the West Point cadets.

If a cartoon character gains favourable recognition and popular acceptance as a symbol of the national spirit it can exert great influence 'Uncle Sam' is among the most prominent examples. Great men and national heroes are powerful stimuli to mass emotions: George Washington, Abraham Lincoln, the Duke of Wellington, Napoleon Bonaparte, Prince Bismarck, and Alexander Nevsky, Mahatma Gandhi are illustrations drawn from five different nations. Great historical events—usually battles—also have symbolic value. Lexington, Gettysburg, Waterloo, Tours, and Poltava are all terms that evoke strong nationalist responses in the appropriate peoples.

The manipulation of nationalist symbols in order to produce the desired popular reaction is a major task of governments today. In this activity they are greatly assisted by the modern techniques of mass communication. Indeed, so necessary to the development of a strong nationalism are the technological means of communicating the patriotic message that it is probable that a people cannot become a nation today unless adequate means of communication exist within a state. Radio, television, motion pictures, pictoral art, and the printed word all can be used to subject the citizen of a modern technological state to a concentrated barrage of nationalist stimuli.

The lesson principally taught by this flow of propaganda is that the individual is part of something greater than himself that his highest mission in life is to perform his public duty, and that all his fellow citizens share this opinion and are expecting him to assume his responsibilities. This sort of programme has two objective: active support for government policy is coupled with minimizing of dissent.

Cycle of Nationalism

Before setting aside the phenomenon of nationalism at this point, we should reflect a little upon the apparently cyclical course it has run throughout history. The record of the rise and decline of nationalism in each people and the course it has followed in its expansion throughout the world both display a certain rhythmic pattern which suggests a possible natural trend.

Liberating Nationalism and Democracy. Originally, as nationalism grew to full stature in revolutionary France and spread outward from its point of origin, it was linked to political democracy and appeared as a liberating force. Its aim was to free national groups from foreign domination and individuals from oppressive social, economic and governmental conditions.

The great nationalist revolutions of the nineteenth century were democratic revolutions as well, or at least were allied to democratic aspirations. By 1914 this movement had reached its peak in Europe. The peace settlements at the end of World War I were based upon the assumption that the revolutionary and upsetting factors in nationalism would be eliminated by satisfying national demands for 'self-determination' and granting democratic government to all such liberated peoples.

The peace-makers of 1919 had overlooked the lesson taught by the successful nineteenth-century movements for the unification of Germany and Italy: nationalism does not need to be allied with democracy to achieve its ends.

Indeed, an authoritarian government might prove to be a more efficient instrument for the accomplishment of national goals, if for no other reasons than its greater unity of organization and concentration of power. The peoples of Europe after 1919, when confronted with a choice between democratic ideals and nationalist goals, tended to choose the latter.

Totalitarian Nationalism. Totalitarian patriotism, involving the complete subjugation of the individual to the will of the state, replaced the 'joyful communion' of individuals with each other which had characterized the nationalism of another period. No longer did nationalism carry democratic connotations; instead it became the ally of authoritarianism.

The nationalist leaders of the 1920's and 1930's—Mussolini, Hitler, Franco, and their lesser imitators—sneered at the democracies as being 'internationalist' and 'cosmopolitan' and drove home their message that only by rigid hierarchical dictatorship could nationalist aims he realized. In the mean, the older variety—liberating nationalism—had continued to spread beyond Europe. India, Turkey, China, and many other states outside western civilization came under its influence, setting in motion chains of circumstances with which the West is contending today. World War II was the logical outgrowth of the development of totalitarian nationalism in Europe (and in Japan) as it came into final collision with the democracies with their less militant national feeling.

Post-World War II: After 1945, the evolution of nationalism continued along the same general lines. New areas of the world became subject to the pressures of liberating nationalism, most significantly Southeast Asia and the Middle East. Other states passed through the liberating phase and entered the period of totalitarian nationalism. China, India, and the USSR are examples of this trend.

Under wartime and postwar conditions, American nationalism came to exhibit some of the 'pathological' characteristics the world came to recognize in Fascist Italy and Nazi Germany: the 'myth of the mass,' the cult of the state, the glorification of conformity, the suppression of dissent, and the vigorous manipulation of symbols to remind American of their duty.

It is too much to claim, however, that the United States has passed into the extreme phase of nationalist orientation: such evidence as exists points rather to a condition in which such a shift could take place, rather than that it has already occurred.

Eclipse of European Nationalism. During the period since

1945, however, a third phase of the cycle has begun in western Europe. The shattering impact of two world wars in thirty years has cooled the ardour of many of the most militant nationalist there. The former enthusiasm for nationalist expansion and the indulging of traditional animosities have largely disappeared; in their place has appeared a broadly based popular movement for international co-operation upon a formal institutionalized basis.

Despite frequent anarchronistic outbursts of the old attitudes, European nationalism today is a far different matter than it was twenty years ago. Something new in nationalism has come into being.

It is too early to say that the prewar variety is forever dead in Europe, but certainly there are strong indications that general disillusionment is widespread with much of the nationalism apparatus.

The German, traditionally the most 'warlike' people in Europe, have been reluctant to take up the burdens of rearmament; the French, the most patriotic people in Europe, have brought the Schuman plan into existence and finally, early in 1955, have agreed to join a rearmed Germany in the defence of Europe; the Italians have abandoned their search for a new Roman Empire in favour of a united Europe.

Future of the Cycle. Does the European experience mean that nationalism is a self-limiting condition? Are there three distinct phases through which nationalism passes naturally: liberating, totalitarian, and declining. If so, does this mean that ultimately, through the growth of wisdom and the accumulation of experience, men will realize the hollowness and futility of the claims of one national group of supremacy and domination over the other.

The decline in European nationalism may prove to be only temporary; furthermore, the giants of contemporary world politics are largely in the grip of extremist attitudes. Inflamed nationalism is a more serious threat to peace today than ever before in history, because the states that are the most belligerent represent a great portion of the power-in-being in the world. If the pathological nationalism of the contemporary world is to cool in its turn, will it require another world war do to it? Will the new nationalism of Southeast Asia and the Middle East (and the yet-to-be-born nationalism of Africa) pass from the first stage to the third without ever menacing world peace by expansionist and totalitarian tendencies?

These critical questions can be answered only at some time in the future when the validity of the cyclical theory has been determined by the processes of history. For the moment we can only point out that at least three distinct forms of nationalism exist in the world at the present time and that their interaction provides much of the subject matter of international politics.

State Personality

The State may be approached either as a legal personality or as a political organization. Legally, the state enjoys a form a fictitious corporate personality, politically, it consists of human beings organized in a particular fashion and serving purpose related to the wants of those individuals.

When, under the pressure of modern state life and the demands of world politics, the idea of corporate personality is blended with the organic reality of human beings, a new concepts is created: the state as a living reality. This idea is of major significance in contemporary international affairs.

The Theory of the Living State

The theory that the state has organic life is an old one. For centuries men have sought for the 'extra-substantial' elements of statehood as they found themselves unsatisfied that the external manifestations of the state—people, territory, and government—captured its inner-most essence. Many schools of philosophy have invested the state with some type of metaphysical significance. The most important of these for the world today is that which finds the state to be living organism.

Till recently, this dogma remained a matter generally

confined to academic discussion. It was not until it allied itself with totalitarian nationalism and became a rallying point for the mass movement of the twentieth century that it came to occupy its present important place as an influence upon world politics.

Today, the nationalist hypothesis of most major states and the point of view assumed by many individuals involve, to some extent, an implicit (sometime explicit) acceptance of the idea that a state is a living organism with its own life cycle and its own destiny.

State Personality vs. Nationalism. To claim that the state is a living organism is an affront to the common sense of most western people. Their sense and their reason tell them that the state is not alive; the state is made up of human beings and the institution they create, and nothing more. Yet, so compelling is modern nationalism that the idea of state personality has already gained acceptance, although sometimes subtly, even among democratic peoples.

The idea of 'national' interest—as a part from popular or individual interest—is the foundation of international politics, yet it is unintelligible without some idea of the reality of the state. This does not deter democracies from pursuing national interest as avidly as do dictatorships. All nationalistic people, free and unfree alike, accept as axiomatic that it is the duty of all individuals to sacrifice their own comfort and security so that the state might prosper.

In their thinking and speaking about world politics, individuals unconsciously reveal the extent to which the idea has taken effect. To Americans, for example, their great enemy is 'Russia'; very few draw any distinction between the Soviet Union as a legal entity, the Russian peoples, and the ruling clique in the government.

It is easier to conceive of world politics as being carried on by organisms called Russia, France, China, and the United States than it is to make careful differentiations among the corporate entities, the living peoples, and the governments.

Popular stereotypes furnish corroboration of this idea; we

hear on all sides such statements as 'the United States is peace-loving', 'Russia is aggressive,' 'France is decadent,' and 'Germany is militaristic'.

Most Americans would deny that they accept the organic hypothesis, but certainly many of its assumptions are incorporated into the American point of view on international politics.

Implications for World Politics

Many implications are there that arise naturally from the concept the organic reality of the state. These bear immediately upon its conduct of foreign policy and the nature of the interstate relationship. We shall consider three: the separate existence of the state, the superior worth of the state, and the role of the individual in the state.

Separate Existence of the State. According to this theory the state has an existence apart from the lives of any or all of its citizens. While humans are mortals, the state is immortal—or at least the life cycle of the state is far longer than that of its people. The independent existence of the state makes it a force over which men have no control; the state moves in response to compulsions—the 'laws' of history, of biology, of logic, and so on—which are cosmic in their influence and, thus, are immune to the machinations of mere humans, The existence of the state transcends them here and now.

Superior Worth of the State. Since state existence is independent of individuals, it is an easy step to reason that the state organism is the highest and most perfect of all organisms, and specifically to claim that individuals must subordinate all their own wishes to those of the state.

It would appear by this logic that the whole (the state) is greater than the sum of its parts (the people), but defenders of the theory insist that this is not true.

The state is more than the sum of the individual citizens, but this does not exhaust its parts; the additional ingredient that makes the state greater than its people is its living personality and reality.

Though it is clear that the state has an existence apart from individuals, individuals are by no means thought to be independent of the state. They are not permitted freely to choose their own role within the society. Using the ready analogy with the human organism, in the state organism individuals are deemed to be cells within the body politic.

Just as individual cells in a body do not question their mission but merely perform their function, so individual human beings have no right to dissent from any state decision. The body cells have specialized functions to perform and each is created for that purpose; in the same way certain men are born to rule, other to fight, and still other to labour. Muscle cells do not attempt to serve as brain cells, and neither should men whose fate it is to serve aspire to be masters in the state. Cells cannot live by themselves, but survive only as part of a larger organism, and individual men can have no real existence of fulfilment outside the state. The whole organism moves and has its being only on command of the brain, the state by command of its government. Many other examples could be cited of the ingenious way in which the organic theory is used to emphasize the subordination of the individual to the living state.

The organic theory, thus, conceives of the state as a self-contained entity which moves as a unity to accomplish its ends in international politics. The state organism functions through its brain, the government; it executes its decision through its body, the people.

In this way foreign policy becomes the province of the ruling few, while the many have no mission except to follow where they are led. The adventurous foreign policies of Nazi Germany, Fascist Italy, and imperial Japan provide instructive illustrations of the probable result of this idea upon world politics.

3

Dynamics of World Politics

The relations of states with each other may assume a broad variety of forms. A government may at the same time be fighting a war with one state, carrying on a diplomatic dispute with another, maintaining close and friendly relations with a third, and virtually isolated from a fourth. War, crisis, friendship and isolation are all equally 'normal' forms of international intercourse; each arises out of appropriate conditions.

This range of possible types of interstate behaviour serves to complicate the study of international relations. From the point of view of the casual observer, the international scene appears to be one of unrelieved confusion. There seems to be no underlying body of principles which govern the conduct of interstate relations, and crisis follow crisis with no apparent causal relationship except the will of statesmen and the workings of blind chance.

States sometimes give the appearance of wandering aimlessly in the pursuit of haphazardly selected objectives and to be continually surprised and taken aback as events work themselves out.

To predict the course of international politics is often a frustrating and unrewarding waste of time and many a citizen has given up the task in disgust. Yet the international order is not as unorganized as might appear at first glance. There are a number of principles, or varying degrees of formalization, which to a large extent actually govern the policies of states and the conduct of statesmen.

Categories of Principles. The first group consists of those that arises as logical deductions from the nature of the nation-state system and which impose certain conditions of existence upon all states. These given international relationships much of their distinguishing character and provide the framework within which all states policies must fit themselves.

The second body of rules includes those principles of action which statesmen follow in carrying on policy as they attempt to adjust to the society of states. Generally they may be thought of as the procedural techniques by means of which policy makers seek to insure the survival of their states and the attainment of the practical maximum of their objectives. In this chapter we shall consider these two sets of principles in order.

Dynamism and the Trend toward Disorder. These rules of organization and procedure are really logical conclusions derived from the assumptions upon which international society is constructed, and are largely independent of the policy of any particular state or of the decisions of any individual statesman.

The premises of international life are many, but in their effect they may be reduced to two: first, the assumption of the monolithic state as an entity complete and whole, implying if not specifying a legal and/or organic reality; second, the assumption that all the states of the world stand in a relationship of sovereign independence and equality to each other.

When states embodying such assumptions enter into intimate and continuous relationships with another, there are certain consequences that immediately rules of interstate life. The system that emerges has two fundamental characteristics: a condition of constant dynamism and change, and a general trend order. In other words, 'normal' international relations—by which is meant a situation in which states follow the logic of their existence—is always changing and is always at least potentially disorderly.

Despite the compelling logic of the conclusions drawn from the nature of the state and the state system, it is nevertheless clear that the course of international politics is not governed entirely by a near-mechanistic determinism.

Human beings, possessed of both reason and will alone reach the decisions and operate the controls that make governments and states act in world affairs. Consequently, the second set of rules which we must consider delineates the principles that govern the decisions and actions of human policy makers.

It is true that their conduct is frequently inhibited by the impact of the conditions of state existence within the society of which they form a part; nevertheless, considerable leeway is permitted human choice in carrying of international relations. As a result of the necessity with which statesmen are faced of carrying on policy in a potentially explosive context, a set of more or less systematized generalizations have been developed with which all successful policy makers are familiar. These aim at specifying the techniques that must be employed by statesmen are to achieve any degree of success of their policies. These derive from the nature of the state system. In general, they are attempts to soften the impact of change and to minimize the trend toward disorder.

Men have not only tried to discover a means of existence within the framework of the society of states; going farther, statesmen for centuries have been seeking to capitalize upon the basic forces of international relations and to turn them to the advantage of mankind. No such effort has yet been completely successful, but each of several of them has had marked influence upon international life in general and upon the course of events within a particular era or eras of history.

An appropriate first premise in the syllogism of international politics is that the relations of states with each other are in a state of constant evolution and change. All social studies that have man as their central object of concern must take account of the notoriously dynamic nature of the human species, but international politics is particularly subject to this caution.

The study is complicated by the relative lack of institutional restraints upon the subjects of its examination, the states themselves. As a result, the student must accept the fact that he is to some extent shooting at a moving target and must adapt his techniques of analysis to that conditions. Let us first examine some of the factors that produce this situation of permanent dynamism.

The Evolution of National Policy. The course of action pursued by a state in attaining its objectives is termed its policy. Although any state is constant in its devotion to its policy, it is not so obvious that the concept of policy is itself dynamic.

The policy the United States is following today is not the same in all its details as that with which it was concerned yesterday; the same is true of all other states with which the United States maintains relations. All the factors that enter into any policy decision are subject both to normal evolution and a sudden change. National interest, national objectives, and national power all defy being frozen into any set pattern.

Another element in the policy process which brings about frequent policy revision is the impact of the actions of other states. We saw earlier how much effort and time any statesman must invest, not in the deliberate pursuit of his own objective, but rather in devising objective response to steps taken by his associates in other states. A policy that may satisfactory so long as it meets only limited resistance often must be drastically altered when it meets firm opposition. The injection of a new issue which requires that corrective action be taken to deal with it serves also to cause policy modifications.

Another factor which also contributes to the constant evolution of national policy might be termed domestic developments. Pronounced political, economic, social, or psychological change within a state inevitably finds expression in foreign policy, thus, adding still another variable. In all these and other ways, we find that policy in a state of permanent evolution is the first explanation of the dynamism of world affairs.

Climate of World Politics. A final variable in world affairs in what we might term the prevailing 'climate.' International affairs, like all forms of politics, is materially affected by the milieu in which events take place and by considerations of time and place. Particular epochs may be favourable to bold and venturesome policies, while others may permit success only to cautious and conservative defences of the status quo.

For example, the period immediately following World War II was one of disorganization and unrest throughout much of the world. This condition of society is usually advantageous to a policy of expansion by a stronger power and the Soviet Union moved rapidly to take any opportunity to capitalize upon it. Much of its postwar success can be explained in these terms. Beginning about 1947, however, the general temper of world opinion had changed. After that time, the defensive policies of the United States began to prove effective in countering Soviet aggrandizement; by 1955 it appeared that the USSR had gone on the defensive. Not only do such changes in 'climate' often occur for unpredictable reasons, but they often take place with relatively little warning and succeed each other with considerable rapidity in today's interdependent world.

Impossibility of Preventing Change. Movement and change are of the essence of the international political process. Failure to recognize and to take account of this essential characteristic has rendered futile many otherwise well-conceived ventures in foreign policy by statesmen of all nationalities. Statesmen have proved to be disposed to fall into this error particularly in the period immediately following a successful and important venture. At the very moment when they have finally achieved an objective of great worth after a long and often perilous struggle, there seems to be a tendency to relax: to assume that the circumstances which produced the victory will endure for ever and that it is unnecessary to take any action to perpetuate them. So long as the nation-state system retains its present characteristics, international politics will not submit to being thus frozen. We need only reflect upon the outcomes of both the great world conflicts of this century to discover historical verification of the persistent dynamism world affairs.

Following the World War I, the victorious Allies constructed with great effort a structure of world relationships which they hoped would guarantee them the permanent enjoyment of the fruits of their victory. Germany and the Central Powers were defeated and reduced either to impotence or to definitely subordinate status; in the League of Nations, furthermore, there existed an instrument which might be used to maintain that relationship. In the immediate postwar period Britain and France (particularly the latter) stubbornly refused to make any but the slightest alternations in the terms of the peace settlement.

It was only later that they learned to their sorrow that the forces of international politics may be temporarily suppressed but they eventually break forth with all the greater violence. Economic depression, resurgent nationalism, and technological advance all combined to render obsolete the settlement that had been won at such cost on the battlefield. The same general pattern re-established itself after World War II. This time, Germany was crushed and dismembered and all its allies had thrown themselves on the mercy of the victors. So complete was the triumph that many people throughout the world felt that at least the forces of freedom and democracy had gained a permanent ascendancy. This dream was dissipated even more rapidly than had been that of 1919. By 1946, the dynamics of international politics had again reasserted themselves and the world was off upon another round of shifting alignments and recurrent crises. Statesmen who seek successful policies must be ever aware of the impossibility of gaining permanent and rigid stability.

The Relations Between States

The sovereign nation-state is the component element of the world society, and by far the greatest number of the contacts that compose international politics take place between them. In appropriate circumstances, however, other forms of political organisation figure in the process. These are of sufficient inherent importance to merit mention at this point, although we must keep in mind that their appearance in the international arena is a periodic rather than a regular matter. Initially we might mention non-sovereign political entities (not, be it noted, ' non-sovereign states.' There is a considerable body of opinion which claims that this latter term is contradictory; to constitute a true state, a political group must be sovereign). These include members of the United Nations such as the Ukrainian Socialist Soviet Republic, creations of the United Nations such as the Free Territory of Trieste, and such de facto governments as those of Indonesia and Israel before the international recognition of their independence. For limited purposes, these groups play a direct part in international affairs and carry on relations with sovereign states.

The second category of special participants in interstate relationships is formed by international organizations of all types. The principal example is of course, the United Nations. Although the organization includes many states, each of which has policy of its own, the United Nations acts frequently as a single entity and conducts affairs with individual states. Often these latter states are United Nations members themselves and thus a single state may appear upon both sides of a negotiation. The ' specialized agencies' of the United Nations (UNESCO, the Intentional Labour Organization, and so on) also carry on direct relations with individual states and thus fall into the same class.

The third group includes blocs of states each of which acts as a unit in pursuing an objective which the members hold in common. If the alliance is sufficiently close and well organized, these states form a single entity and any relationship between the group and an outside state is as if only two states were involved.

The European Coal and Steel Community (ECSC) and the North Atlantic Treaty Organization (NATO) are two examples of such blocs which in reality deal with non-members upon a state-to-state basis. Whenever any of these special organizational types do have contact with sovereign states (or with each other). The following general principles apply as completely as in the case of only two states.

The Nature of the Interstate Relationship. Here, we will briefly examine the principal features of the relationship that arises between such states. In the first place, each participant in world politics is proceeding in response to internal motivations; interest, objectives, and policy all arise in response to stimuli the origin of which is within the state. Secondly, each state possesses certain increments of power with which it supports its policy. Third, the society in which state move and carry on their relations is structurally incomplete.

Large areas of state action are completely free from institutional regulation, while such rules as exist are often vague or else lack mechanism of enforcement. A fourth factor which affects this relationship is the fact that there is no agreement today among all states upon any single moral code by which to judge the propriety of state action.

The relationship between states which derives from these conditions necessarily reflects them. States approach each other as free agents with no inherent reason for mutual confidence. Each is required by the system to view the others as actual or potential competitors; each is prepared to advance its own cause at the expense of the others and to seek to prevent them from doing same.

An agreement is based upon a coincidence of interest and may be great or small, long-lasting or temporary, depending upon how extensively and how long the respective national interests happen to remain in harmony. Which of the states gain the bulk of its objectives is determined largely by the interplay of power factors. It must be stressed that within the present structure of the nation-state system, the *criteria of morality and justice* which we in the Western world accept as guides to private conduct are to a great extent irrelevant. States, by the very circumstances of their existence, are obliged to accept different standards.

The relations between particular pairs or groups of states have often been friendly for long periods of time and real harmony has marked their contracts. The great degree of cordiality in Canadian-American relations since the middle of the nineteenth century is a good example of this type of relationship. Even this felicitous arrangement, however, when examined closely, reveals the characteristics mentioned above. With the best will in the world, even such similarly situated states as Canada and the United States have been unable completely to escape the logical consequences of their existence as sovereign political entities.

Dissent, disagreement and occasional open dispute between them upon numerous issues serves to remind us all that each is a sovereign state with the primary goal of serving its own best interest.

The Forms of the Interstate Relationship

(1) *Hostility.* The relationship between states covers a wide gamut of forms in its constantly changing evolution. At one extreme is the relationship of extreme hostility, including war. This is rooted in a direct clash of vital interests between the states involved, and is marked by the open, direct, and usually unlimited mutual application of violence.

It arises when states have been unable to discover a formula for settling a dispute, and the only means left open to them in such a situation to achieve their objectives is to attempt to coerce their opponent into submission. If war exists between two states, hostility extends to every point of contact between them and no other basis for supporting a relationship is possible.

If, conflict does not reach the point of violence, relations between the states may be hostile only in certain areas and upon certain issues, while remaining cordial and even friendly in others.

(2) *Friendship.* At the other extreme, an interstate relationship may be friendly and marked by close policy co-operation. In this case, an identity of interest exists, either upon a particular issue or upon a more broadly based general programme. At the very least, friendly relations between states indicate a lack of fundamental disagreement.

Cooperative affirmative action is more likely when active agreement exists upon an issue sufficiently important to motivate concrete policy steps, but friendship may be just as close if it arises out of a mere lack of grounds of disagreement. In any case, hostility or friendship between states is directly proportional to the degree to which their interests conflict.

Balance: Somewhere in between the two extremes are found most of the actual relations of states. Clashes of interest are normal, but so is some degree of agreement; the result is some form of dynamic balance which reflects the conflict-agreement mixture. State prosecute their differences with other states, but the lengths to which they will go in the struggle are limited by such agreement as exists upon other policy matters. The converse is also true; co-operation upon the basis of identity of interest is usually incomplete because of the existence of other areas of controversy.

The Web of Relationships

The State in the Multi-state System. The state, exists within a system along with all its fellows. Let us for a moment consider how it fits itself into this framework. Each state has a policy derived from its national interest and consisting of a set of objectives and a programme for their attainment. It also has a certain amount of power with which to gain those objectives. Each state determines for itself which objectives it will seek, in what priority they will be arranged, how it will go about attaining them, and the power commitments necessary and appropriate for the purpose. So far can it go on its own. From this point forward the degree of success or failure it enjoys is determined to a large measure by the fact that it is one among a number of similarly minded states. Once a state decides upon a policy and sets it into motion, it immediately comes into contact with many other states, each doing the same thing.

As each state pursues its objectives with regard to all its fellows, it attempts to arrange matters within each of these relationships to its satisfaction. This necessitates paying close attention to each of them, making advances towards its goal when possible, standing fast when desirable, and retreating when necessary and expedient.

A state that finds itself at a power disadvantage in a particular relationship must usually either give ground there or weaken its effort elsewhere in order to gain the additional power necessary to stabilizes the first situation; a state that finds its opponent weakening may increase its own pressure so as to force a victory or else may reduce its own effort, restore the balance and employ the ensuing surplus of power elsewhere. If the last course is chosen, new situational changes are thus brought about which call in turn for new corrective measures.

It must be remembered that each state maintains some sort of relations with nearly all the other seventy odd members of the nation-state system, and in doing so it exerts pressure upon and receives pressure exerted by each of them. The multi-state system is a complex and intricate web of dynamic relationship, each materially affecting all the others. As a result, the task of any statesman is to pick his way through these complexities with skill and direction sufficient to gain the practical maximum of his policy objectives.

Absolute success in international politics is so rare as to be practically nonexistent. No state do more than come close to reaching its policy goals; the system itself intervenes to prevent most solutions from being truly clear-cut.

Any state in serving the objectives it has laid down for itself is beset by so many interruptions and irrelevancies—most of which arise from the nature of the system—it is seldom that it can devote itself single-mindedly to the fulfilment of its own plans.

Chain Reaction of Policy Change. The results of even a minor policy change by any state usually extend far beyond the immediate issue.

As soon as any state makes a modification in its policy as it affects any other state, the latter seeks to bring its own programme into harmony with the situation. This in turn presents other states with different circumstances, which they in turn must meet by making policy shifts of their own.

Still other states are affected at this point and more policy alterations take place—all of which reminds us of the concentric ripples that radiate out from the point at which a dropped stone struck the surface of a placid pool of water. In this way each policy change tends to touch off a chain reaction of adjustment to it. Some of these may be slight in the first place, but so delicately most statesmen calculate in allocating their available power that the effect of any policy modification tends to increase in a geometric proportion.

Each state involved in any of the chain reactions—and in today's interdependent world nearly every state is ultimately drawn into the process—meets each such set of new conditions one at a time and in a way determined by its own situation and the demands of its national interest.

The changes follows each other, often with bewildering rapidity. What is more, these chain reactions often affect each other. Sometimes they neutralize each other and particular states may be able to adjust to new conditions without making any significant policy changes at all; sometimes they double up in their effect and states must execute virtual policy reversals in order to keep abreast of a drastically altered set of conditions.

Most of the time the interaction of the various patterns is not so clear or so extreme as has been suggested. Instead, their impact is relatively intensified or diluted as the result of their concurrence. In any case, the nature of international politics is such that each state must always be prepared to modify its policy in great or in small measure in response to changes in circumstances brought about in the first instance by a policy change made by some other side.

United States Trade Policy and the Chain Reaction. In 1951, the Congress of the United States enacted the Battle Act, designed as cut off trade between the free world and the Soviet sphere by denying American aid to any state engaged in trading with Iron Curtain states. This was actually an intensification of an already decided policy—an increase in the power we were exerting upon our allies. This policy change set in motion a chain reaction.

Each of our allies, faced with this new move on the part of the United States, sought to react to it as best it could in terms of its own situation. Great Britain, for example, found the new American attitude distinctly unfavourable to itself, both in the area of Anglo-American relations and in dealing with the Soviet.

Diplomatic representations were made to the United States; consultations were held with other adversely affected states; the possibilities of an entirely new line of procedure based upon the termination of American aid were explored. All of these moves added up to a counterbalancing increase in the power Britain was in turn applying to the United States.

Britain adjusted to a new American policy, and its programmes in other policy areas were in turn affected. Its Soviet policy was modified, its relations with its fellows in the alliance of the free world were overhauled and made closer under the stimulus of a common problem, and its economic policy sought to make up for the loss of its trade behind the Iron Curtain.

The states affected by the last group of derivative policies were in turn confronted by new conditions in dealing with Britain. The Soviet Union, for example, redoubled its efforts to split the Western alliance by tempting Britain with ever more attractive offers of trade agreements; in doing so, however, it was in its turn obliged to prepare itself to modify its economic relations with its satellites and to soften much of its propaganda campaign against U.K.

And so the process continued, involving all the states initially affected by the passage of the Battle Act; each reacted to new conditions by policy adjustment.

There is no need to go into further details at this point about the specific issue: it seemed to have reached resolution of at least one phase in late 1953 and early 1954, when the United States government officially relaxed the ban on trading in non-strategic materials behind the Iron Curtain. The incident illustrates the fact, however, that the consequences of a single policy change by any state cannot in practice be kept confined. Reaction to change is inevitable, and its ultimate ramifications are almost impossible to predict. It is for this reason that every government keeps a watchful eye upon all developments in the whole globe arena of world politics.

Anarchy of Interstate Life

The society in which the sovereign state has its existence is one that by very nature is potentially disorderly. In contrast, a domestic social life is marked by orderly behaviour, the promulgation of general accepted rules, and the progressive elaboration of the institutional structure. These characteristics are only partly present in the contacts that states have with each other. Consequently, the nation-state system moves according to a different set of principles from that of private society. To draw analogies between domestic and international life is deceptive and misleading unless the differences between the two systems are kept clear.

Philosophers and political scientists use the term anarchy to describe the situation within a society in which there is no government, no agency to enforce order, and no universally applicable rules of behaviour.

Limited Effect of Institutions. The institutions of international life—the formalized agencies that embody moral principles and rules of conduct are incomplete and of limited effect. International organizations of various types exist which include states as members and which pursue their particular objectives with varying degrees of success.

Membership in these is voluntary on the part of any state, however, and each member in practice determines for itself the degree to which its conduct is affected by the dictates of the organization. One need recall only the uneven response given by members of the United Nations to the call for military action in Korea to become convinced that the organization is not yet the controlling element in international politics.

International law as an institution is also relatively weak and feeble compared to its domestic counterpart. The scope of the law is restricted; several critical forms of state conduct do not come within its provisions. Its enforcement mechanisms, when present at all, are weak. States obey international law upon the occasions and to the extent that it conforms to their national interest to do so.

The institution of diplomacy, the formal mechanism of interstate contact and communication, draws its validity from its expediency rather than from its institutional maturity. When a state chooses to employ some other channel of communication and has the power to make itself heard, it is free to do so; no automatic sanctions exist to prevent or punish the violation of the institutional framework. It would therefore appear that states are not in any fundamental way restricted in their international conduct by the existence of any institutional structure, but instead feel themselves to be legally and morally free agents—a basically anarchic point of view.

There is no logical reason for a state to feel any real sense of fundamental obligation or respect to any entity outside itself. The law and the philosophy of statehood in international relations make the state form an end in itself. There is no room in the concept for any higher or outside loyalty.

It is questionable to think of the terms 'international society' or 'world community' as having meaning when applied to the sovereign states in the world. For a society or community to exist, there must be some form of consensus, some form of recognition of a mutual obligation to the group. There must be a willingness on the part of individuals upon occasion to submerge their private concerns by the appropriate requirements of the society. There must usually also be some agreed-upon authority to enforce decisions in the name of the collective whole. In the relations between sovereignties, no such sense of community obligation can logically be presumed to exist. The notion of the national interest is an all-inclusive one which demands the complete commitment of the state to its service.

Each state is therefore so immersed in the service of its own interest that little room is left for a sense of duty to be applied to the whole group.

The pattern of international politics offers many examples of this idea. One of the most recent afforded by the question of European unification, which has been a major issue since 1945. The idea of a unified Europe is one of great logical force and has the additional advantage of being in harmony with existing conditions.

From 1947 to 1955, aided by pressure from the United States and a common fear of the USSR, progress toward European unification was made in number of areas.

France has been obstinate in obstructing the plans because it feels that its interest demands military supremacy over Germany; Italy seeks satisfaction of certain territorial claims; West Germany is ever raising the question of German unification; Britain refuses to become a full partner in Europe—thus impeding and almost stopping further advance—because of its reluctance to give up its area of independence in world affairs and its position as leader of the Commonwealth of Nations.

All have been eager to gain American support of their own policies and have given some measure of consideration to American interest in European union in order to United States backing in return. But the limited success of the European movement up to the present—despite the fact that its ultimate prospects are bright—is due primarily to the inability or the refusal of the European states themselves to recognize a duty or a loyalty to anything greater than themselves.

Self-help. In a highly organized society there are institutions to assist the individual in coping with situations beyond his strength. Though law and by means of private organizations, the social group guarantees to private citizens a measure of rights and freedoms and stands behind him if these are invaded.

No such situation can be assumed in the state system. The only logical method open to a state to attain its objectives and to secure redress of injuries is to employ its own strength.

Self-help in crisis situations, unusual in private life, is a common and routine procedure in international politics. The only rights and freedoms is the possession of which a state can feel truly secure are those it is physically capable of defending. This necessarily means that the power inequalities of states are usually faithfully reflected in their respective areas of rights and freedoms.

Furthermore, each state may determine for itself what measures are appropriate in any situation and—despite some attempts of formulating legalistic restraints—no presently exists which effectively links that freedom.

It has sometimes been claimed, for example, that the United Nations Charter has made war illegal. Even if this point be granted, however, then still remains the unsolved problem of how this judgment could be enforced against a possible violator without first winning a war against it.

Many of the rules of international conduct were themselves initially laid down by powerful states in a moment of victory with the basic objective of legitimizing a policy that had proved successful.

Such were the rules making aggressive warfare a crime punishable by death which were handed down by the 'war crimes' tribunals in Germany and Japan after World War II. This fact tends to make international affairs a demonstration of the ancient thesis that 'might makes right'.

The central feature of the anarchy of international politics is the right of the state to go to war any time it decides such action is expedient. The employment of force without limit in order to coerce other states into agreement is a logical derivation arising from the nature of interstate relations. War is therefore considered to be a normal—although often undesirable and unwise—technique of policy.

All attempts to organize international relations upon a basis of orders and they have upto to this time come to brief upon this central idea. As long as they feel that they can not trust any outside agency to give them complete fulfilment of what they deem to be their legitimate interests, they are not going to give up their power to enforce their rights themselves.

In this way, the power of states and their willingness and ability to use it becomes the ultimate determinant of most international intercourse, particularly in times of crisis.

When states disagree, the only procedure that will produce definitive solutions within the peculiar framework of the state system is the mutual application of elements of power by the states involved. No external mechanisms that the world has thus far seen have proved capable of ending such a struggle in any clear-cut way.

Hobbes's Vision of Anarchy. One of the most famous evocations of the consequences of anarchy was made by Thomas Hobbes, the seventeenth-century British philosopher. In Leviathan (1651), he sought to justify the institution of civil government as the only way by which man could escape chaos. To make his point more effective, he drew a vivid picture of what human social intercourse would be like if there were of civil authority to enforce order.

This 'state of nature', said he, would be a miserable existence; he called it a 'war of all against all.' Man, driven by his appetites an instinct of acquisitiveness, would be engaged in constant conflict with his fellows. Self-preservation was the basic human motivation; that accomplished, man would turn to the service of his physical and psychic well-being. He would have only his physical strength and his native wit to aid him in this purpose.

He could turn for assistance neither to organized society (which would not, under these conditions, have any existence) nor to his fellows (except for those particular designs which coincided with the interests of certain other individuals, and then only for the duration of such agreement). There would be no rational basis for any relationship of trust with his fellow men, for all would be competitors for the same rewards.

The result would be incessant hostility. Each man would

enjoy such personal security and rewards as he was powerful enough to gain and retain, and each would be racked by fear of violence and death as he eked out his allotted span.

From this unhappy existence man could be liberated only by the creation of a central governmental authority to protect all against all.

Without stretching the analogy, we can discover a close resemblance between Hobes's classic vision of anarchy and the theoretical premises upon which international politics are built. The assumpiton of hostility, arising from the absence of a common ground of understanding and procedure underlies much of the basic approach of states to each other.

No central governing body, no generally respected rules, and no all-inclusive moral control sovereign states. The principle of action inherent in the state system is *sauve qui peut*—every man for himself.

Power Politics

The system of states, being a regime posited upon a partly systematized anarchy, takes its driving force from the only principle of action appropriate in such a society. With no socially sanctioned principles of right and wrong provide guides to correct procedure, the international political process can be and often is summed up in a single simple phrase: power politics. The germ of the idea is expressed in the aphorism: ' States do what they can and suffer what they must.' This is the lesson of power politics.

The Determination of Policy. Each state determines for itself both its policy objectives and its techniques. There are no objectives that are in themselves wrong or immoral in any absolute sense; a state is free to attempt world conquest or world revolution with no sense of moral restraint, provided only that its people feel that such action is in the national interest. The selection of appropriate techniques for attaining objectives is also done unilaterally; and means that promises success may be adopted, up to and including total war.

It must be stressed that these decisions about objectives and techniques are reached within the framework of government of each state. In international politics there are no external agencies, like those in private life, whose impact must be taken into account in every such decision. The law that always prohibits antisocial objectives and the policeman who punishes antisocial action are equally minor in their effect upon states. Prospects of success or failure, interpreted in the light of the national interest, provide the guides to policy which states actually follow.

To say that the selection of objectives and techniques goes on entirely within a state is not, however, to say that it takes place in a complete vacuum. All statesmen recognize and act upon a set of restraints. These are new: wholly concrete and usually are not verbalized, but they nonetheless delineate the real area of freedom enjoyed by a state in making any policy decision.

These restraints are represented by the existence of all other states, each of which is engaged in the identical process of seeking the achievement of its objectives and the satisfaction of its national interest. This means that any policy decision made by a state will inescapably meet some degree of freedom from a number of the states affected by it.

Any action programme, as an essential part; a judgment of the power necessary for success. The probability of meeting superior hostile power serves as an immediate limitation upon the freedom of choice of states. Superior power is still the only final arbiter in the state system and it serves as one of the controlling mechanisms is shaping the course of world politics.

Settlement of Disputes. The principles of power politics are seen at their clearest in the settlement of an international dispute. When two states become involved in a controversy, the final resolution of the dispute is arrived at in terms of power.

The merits of the respective cases and considerations of legal or moral rights are irrelevant to the final outcome, except insofar as they themselves are factors of power on one side or the other.

No questions are actually settled in any rational sense by the operation of the state system except those involving power. World War II, for example, did not prove that Hitler was morally or legally wrong, nor did it prove that the United Nations had fought in defence of a set of absolutely applicable moral precepts.

Nothing was finally decided about the relative merits of dictatorship and democracy, or of authoritarianism and freedom. All that was established was that the military machine commanded by Hitler and his associates was insufficiently powerful to withstand the onslaught of the forces arrayed against it.

This verdict, although clear-cut and providing a base for future policy, was independent of the emotional involvements of individuals and of any moral judgment binding upon the collectivities called states. The haste with which the former enemies have resumed close relations and with which the victorious alliance dissolved after the war serves to underscore this verdict.

Power politics means in practice that international disputes tend to be settled in terms of the relative power applied by each party. If a sufficient preponderance of power be mustered by one state, a fairly clear victory is gained; if the opposing forces are sufficiently well balanced so as to make a forced triumph impossible or inexpedient, some compromise is arranged which reflects the relative strength of the disputants. This generalization is equally applicable to a violent conflict or to a diplomatic controversy.

The Competitive System

The Competitive Approach. The logic of the state system necessitates that states approach each other in an atmosphere of competition. Competition and conflict may not be evident in any particular interstate relationship, but they underlie all of them any serve to govern the strategy and tactics of states in conducting their policies.

The principle cause of the competitive approach of states is found in the egocentric nature of the state institution which we noted above. Each state plays its part in world affairs as a means of satisfying its own desires and in any situation in such a manner as to turn it to the maximum advantage.

A second premise which adds to this atmosphere of competition is that most national objectives are logically absolute. States are by nature insatiable there is no rational end to a policy of security, prestige, or ideology except world domination.

Later in this chapter we shall see how statesmen to discover and lay down practical limits to these absolutist drives. For the moment, however, it suffices to point out that the nature of the interstate relationship makes it inherently a competitive one.

A striking example of how states react to new situations in a competitive way was furnished by the rapid sequence of events of Iran during August 1953. The internal political convulsion through which that state passed and resented one of the sudden and unexpected twists of history which required immediate adjustment on the part of nearly every state.

All the powers analyzed the *coup d'etat* of Prime Minister Mossadegh, the flight of the Shah, the almost immediate counter-revolution, the return of the Shah and Mossadegh's arrest in terms of the impact of these events upon their own long-range and absolute objectives.

Some states gained an advantage by the turn of events some were injured; most were unable to discover immediately how they had fared and consequently avoided making over hasty commitments.

The relations of the major powers to each other were materially affected. The United States found the change in Iran's government to its linking; with a pro-Western ruler once again in command there, the United States withdraw some of the power with which it had been supporting its Iranian policy and use it to increase the pressure it was exerting upon the Soviet world.

Great Britain, hoping for an end to the annoying dispute with Iran over the expropriation and nationalization of the anglo-

Iranian Oil Company looked to an end to that quarrel and to the opportunity to play a larger role elsewhere in the Middle East.

This improved position would strengthen the hand with the Soviet on the one hand and the United States on the other. The accuracy of British judgment seemed to be confirmed when, a few months later, diplomatic relations were resumed with Iran after a long period of suspension. The oil dispute was finally settled during the summer of 1954.

The USSR, on its part, found itself at a disadvantage as a result of the change of government in Iran. The new ruling group was clearly anti-Soviet (Mossadegh had been, at least, benevolently neutral in the cold war). Russian policy was obliged to face the alternatives of employing direct coercion upon the new regime or else permitting a significant impairment of its position in Iran and the entire Middle East.

In either case its position with regard to the West was weakened. Each of the three major powers analyzed the Iranian crisis in the light of its own objectives and policy and sought to extract the maximum advantage for itself.

Conflict and Agreement. We already know that the guide followed by each state in international politics is its own concept of national interest. When the national interests of any two states fix upon the identical objective and each seeks its attainment, a situation of international conflict is created. When interests do not clash but instead coincide, harmony and agreement exist.

Because of the absoluteness of national interest and the inevitably competitive pursuit of national objectives, we should logically expect conflict to be the most common climate of international relations. To take just one example, so long as each state conceives security as an objective to be materially attained, no other relationship than conflict is possible as each state seeks to achieve security on its own terms.

Competition, our economists assure us, is the life of trade; in international relations it is the life of politics as well. It is the basis upon which the system is constructed. Were some other factor the governing force in the constant intercourse of states, the story of international affairs would be entirely different.

Competition in Practice. States do not, in their corporate capacity, 'trust' each other as do individuals; each of them regards all the others as competitives and potential adversaries. The logic of national sovereignty does not allow any state to view with equanimity the progress of any other state toward the attainment of any of its absolute goals. All must be concerned over any increase in the power of any of the others. No matter where such improvement in the status of any state may be directed at the moment, there is no reason for any of its associates to assume that this increased power may not some day be pointed at them.

Consequently, as soon as any state succeeds in improving its position in any perceptible and significant way, one of the chain reactions we discussed earlier immediately sets in. Every other state in a position to do so strives either to strengthen its own position in proportion or else to weaken the newly powerful state in some other way so as to restore the relationship to something like its former dimensions.

All of the available resources of policy are usually thrown behind this attempt at readjustment; it is a matter of great urgency for most states and becomes often the first order of business. The possible means are many: military (rearmament), political (new alliances), economic (discriminatory trade practices), or psychological (propaganda campaigns). If it proves to be impossible to redress the balance, all the states involved must thereupon make major policy changes which reflect the altered power relationship.

Competition and Atomic Control. The postwar manoeuvring of the major powers on the question of the international control of atomic energy and atomic weapons provides an instructive example of this process. At the end of the war in 1945, the United States enjoyed a 'monopoly' of atomic knowledge, at least as far as the manufacture of military feasible atomic bombs was concerned.

The United Kingdom and the USSR, to say nothing of the rest of the world, were disquieted by this development; despite our assurances of good intentions, they found American leadership in atomic weapons to be a cause of insecurity. They undertook several policies in an attempt to rectify the situation.

All sought some form of international control over atomic energy which would have freed them from the danger of American employment of the bomb as a policy weapon, and at the same time would have given them access to American technical information and production techniques. The United States, in its turn, refused to part with its information without gaining a corresponding policy advantage over both Britain and the Soviet.

We advocated a form of international control (the 'Baruch plan') which would have permitted us to construct bombs until such time a world-wide atomic regulation would have forbidden the use of atomic power for military purposes. The adoption of this proposal would have enabled us to maintain our continued power advantage over the USSR and Britain.

This was totally unacceptable to the USSR, even though the fundamental harmony of interest between Britain and the United States persuaded the British to accept it. The Soviet Union and the United Kingdom both intensified their own research and development programmes following the failure of this initial effort to discover a formula of control; by 1951 both had exploded bombs of their own. Now it was the turn of the United States to be disturbed.

Although American leadership was yet unchallenged, the fact that other states had mastered the scientific and technical problems of bomb manufacture necessarily represented a wakening of the United States power position. The search for international control over atomic power thereupon took on a new dimension for Americans; it was no longer a problem of confining the USSR to a position of inferiority, but instead one of seeking to neutralize a growing power factor in the position of the principal adversary of the United States.

As a result, in 1953 the United States made a new proposal for international atomic control, focused upon the peaceful exploitation of atomic power instead of upon its military aspects; the American government kept urging its adoption during the next two years. An international conference on the peaceful use of atomic energy, in which Communist and free world scientists exchanged information, was held in Geneva in the summer of 1955. This was the first concrete result of the new American policy.

In the meantime, the lesser states found themselves trapped in a steadily deteriorating situation as the great powers made more and more progress in atomic weapons. There is no logical reason for small powers to trust any of the three world leaders with atomic bombs, or any one of them more than the other two. Accordingly, they are reacted in several directions.

In the first place, many—notably India—have redoubled their efforts to gain some effective form of international control. Secondly, several of them—including especially France—have been devoting increasing amounts of money and manpower to a feverish research programme of their own.

In the third place, those in a position to do so have attempted to use their bargaining power to secure some rectification of the atomic balance. France, for example, attempted repeatedly to make its inclusion in the atomic power—a price for its approval of German rearmament.

The problem of atomic energy is only one manifestation of the competitive system of world politics; it is a basic characteristic of the system in which any advantage gained by one state sets off a search for compensating gains by the others.

The Pressure-Counter-Pressure Relationship. The state relations between any two states is therefore determined by the interaction of two opposing current of force. We have already seen that states approach each other competitively and that no international institution exists which can guarantee the outcome of any particular dispute. As between any two states, there is a two-directional flow of power.

Each state is engaged in a constant process of applying power to all its associates—in some cases direct and in considerable quantity, in others indirect and in small amount—and at the same time it is itself the object of power applied by all other states.

That balance that is struck between the two flows of power and the resistance each meets determine the over-all climate of relations between any such states.

Of course, it is impossible to measure the mutual relationships of the different factors of power with anything like mathematical exactitude. Too many imponderables enter into the judgments of statesmen and no policy maker is able to govern his conduct exclusively by the power exerted upon him from beyond the boundaries of his state.

The existence of the pressure-counter-pressure relationship, however, provides the point of departure in the process of policy making by all rational statesmen.

Power in War and Peace. This dichotomy applies in all international relationships. It is of course most obvious in time of war, when each combatant uses all the political, economic, psychological, and military power at its command in order to force compliance with its wishes. The verdict of war is delivered clearly in terms of the relative power applied.

The only significant difference between a warlike relationship and a peaceful one, however, is the particular means employed. The mental orientation, the objectives, and the principles of action are identical: to coerce the opponent into agreement. Non-violent struggles do not go to the extremes of war, and compromise upon the basis of relative commitments of power is usually easier to arrange.

Intra-alliance Relationships. In international politics there are many close and 'harmonious' relations between particular states, but even these are susceptible to the influence of competition and mutual pressure. Mutuality of interest explains co-operative action. No international agreements in history have been closer or more binding than some of the defensive alliances worked out by states that have felt themselves menaced by a common enemy.

The greatest and most inclusive of these was the United Nations Organization, the 'grand alliance' of World War II. Yet even this one—among the most successful international groupings of all time—was marked by constant bickering among its members and was not able to survive to make a lasting peace.

A single overriding interest—a fear of the common enemy, the powers—brought together a number of otherwise ill-assorted states. Agreement of interest upon one point, however, even such an important one, did not carry with it agreement upon all. Each member of the alliance was wanted the war for its own purposes and was pursuing its own future advantage. Each had its own version of what it wanted the postwar world to be like, and each attempted to influence the conduct of the war in that direction.

Great Britain, for example, sought to persuaded the other allies to make the major European effort of the war in the area of the Balkans in order to preserve its own influence and power there after the fighting ended. The USSR insisted upon a second front in Europe long before the War was prepared for such action; this would have relieved some of the pressure upon the Red armies and simultaneously weakened the West in the postwar world.

The United States, seeking the earliest possible end to the European phase of the struggle so as to be able to shift its emphasis to the Pacific, insisted upon a cross-channel invasion as the cheapest and most direct method of destroying the enemy. Other allies—France, the Netherlands, China, and others—also sought to influence strategic and tactical decisions to their own advantage.

The alliance proved unable to outlast the crisis that had brought it into existence. Once the single common purpose of all the various governments had been accomplished by the defeat of the Axis, the national interests of the allies fell again into their mutually competitive relationships, and the alliance disintegrated.

It was replaced by new alignments more in harmony with the situation that prevailed after the war. It is a truism of diplomacy that a military alliance endures only as long as the crisis responsible for its creation continues to concern the states involved.

Degrees of Competitiveness. Although logically the requirements of the state system demand that states be absolutely competitive in their relations with one another, in practice the level of intensity of the actual conflict between them varies among different states and between the same states at different times. The competition between states waxes and wanes in direct proportion to the degree to which their interests clash. If no conflict of interest in relations are either nonexistent (a logical but improbable condition) or harmonious.

At times, harmony of interest upon particular issues may be so great as to enable states to forego their normally competitive approach. It was, for example, to the real interest of the United States that its European allies be strengthened after 1947.

On the one hand, if a direct collision involves matters of vital importance to both states, the inevitable conflict may reach the peak of war. As concepts of interest held by states in executing their policies involve in response to internal developments and the course of history the degree of competitiveness between particular states may change, either intensifying or relaxing.

Sometimes long-standing hostilities dissolve, as was the case between Britain and France after 1900 as both were menaced by an expanding Germany. Sometimes new hostilities are born as interests expand; the suddenly emergent conflict between the United State's and the Soviet Union after 1945 was the direct outgrowth of the radical expansion in interest which both states experienced as a result of World War II.

Techniques of Stability

In the preceding section we attempted to demonstrate that the assumptions upon which the state system is grounded operate upon states to direct their activities in particular directions. However, even after it is admitted that constant dynamism and a trend toward disorder are the theoretical principles upon which the system depends, it remains obvious that in fact international relations do not always display these characteristics in any extreme measure.

Movement, evolution, and change do actually take place in the relations of states, but in practice it is rate that they occur as frequently and extensively as is theoretically possible: instead, both their pace and their direction are subject to considerable control.

The trend toward disorder is usually confined within fairly clear limits through the efforts of statesmen. The collapse of orderly international relationships—an event logically to be expected to occur often in terms of the theoretical base of the state system—in instead today viewed today by most people as a catastrophe whose avoidance is a matter of first importance.

Indeed, when one considers the inescapable first principles of international life and the possible consequences that might flow from them, the relatively high incidence of peace and orderly process which obtains in international relations is a tribute to the dedication and in tenuity of most of the statesmen who guide the destiny of states.

In general their task of preserving order may be thought of as a limiting one. If the logic of international relations should be permitted to reach its ultimate development, the relations between states would resemble the concept of anarchy. The dynamic forces of international life cannot be completely eliminated so long as the state system retains its historic development of organization.

This being the case, the rational statesman seeks to work out the details of his policy in harmony with these postulates. He attempts to capitalize upon those factors in the international situation which operate to his advantage and to control and limit those which are unfavourable. The impact of change is thereupon minimized and the greater share of interstate contacts gains a reasonable degree of systematization.

It might almost be said that the forces of international politics are self-neutralizing. The closer disaster comes within any particular context, the greater the effort put forth by statesmen to ward it off. In this endeavour they have several techniques of stability to aid them.

The Rule of Expediency

Perhaps the best—and certainly the most enduring—of all the guides to practical statesmanship ever written is The Prince (1513), by the Nicolo Machiavelli Renaissance figure. Although written early in the sixteenth century, his maxims of prudence and force are as applicable to contemporary conditions as they were to the era of the Renaissance.

The general lesson taught by this little book is the first of the great techniques which all statesmen must respect and apply. It may be termed the 'rule of expediency', always to do what is expedient and to refrain from doing what is inexpedient. No more inclusive and efficacious imperative could be imagined for insuring state success in international relations and the preservation of the structure of peace.

To comprehend the nature of expediency, it is vital a policy maker be sensitive to all situational factors that affect him and his government. Other statesmen misjudge the expediency of a particular course under existing conditions and thus they err about where the maximum advantage for their state lies.

In such cases international crises occur with potentially disastrous results. Sometimes the impact of other political or psychological forces lead them to ignore practicality in policy and to undertake risky and adventuresome programmes. Nevertheless, the rule of expediency is perhaps the most revealing single idea aiding in the comprehension of the behaviour of statesmen.

Relativism of International Politics. The state is morally its own excuse for being in any international sense; it requires moral justifications other than those which it provides for itself.

The only concepts of 'good' and 'bad' which have any relevance to the international conduct of the state are relative to its success or failure in attaining its objectives. Any policy that succeeds in advancing national interest is a good policy; any policy that, for whatever reason, fails to reach its objective is by that fact a bad one. No more relativist philosophy could be imagined.

It has proved particularly difficult for Americans to grasp this idea, because it runs directly counter to our native political philosophy, the doctrine of natural rights. Our ideology is grounded upon a series of premises which we hold to be true and of universal moral application.

This absolutist doctrine has served us well at home; accordingly, we tend to assume that international politics also is organized upon a series of absolute dogmas of morality. Many of the rude shocks which we have felt since 1945 have been due to our natural expectation that the principles of political democracy would be applicable at the international level. This has simply proved not to be the case; instead, the conduct of states is determined by a highly flexible relativism.

Part of the confusion to which many individuals are subject in thinking about world affairs is due to the fact that they fail to realize the irrelevance of private moral principles in considering the relationships of states. In point of fact, the corporate state does not govern its international conduct by the Judiac-Christian code of ethics to which most individuals in the Western world subscribe.

It might be a better and more orderly world if states did so, and perhaps we shall know stability only when statesmen apply the same standards to their official policy that they do to their private lives. In practice, however, states do not seek to accomplish the absolute moral right and to free the wrong as these concepts are formulated by any ethical religious code.

Whatever they may be attempting to accomplish at the moment is 'right' and 'good' at that time; whenever a new line of policy is selected, it becomes 'right' and 'good' in its turn.

This is not to say that governments never espouse the cause of private morality; indeed, many of them often do. When a state's policy leads it to advocate policy in harmony with principles of private right and justice, however, it does so because of its belief that such action is in service of the national interest.

When interest diverges from morality, few statesmen hesitated. They usually continue to adhere to the guide of interest, and abandon (although sometimes regretfully) the teachings of the private moral code.

It would be inaccurate to imply that the state is a completely amoral entity with no concern for any moral principles. Actually, in international relations the state serves as the creator of a morality of its own, and it policy is shaped by the teaching of a doctrine of which it is the principal architect.

This 'state-morality' is, as Machiavelli pointed out, logically disassociated from private ethics. The objectives of the state organization are different from those of private persons and its conduct must therefore be measured by different standards.

In modern political life, the state from looms large in the activity sphere of individuals, and it is inescapable that under such conditions state-oriented and state manipulated codes of behaviour should come to gain wide acceptance despite their seeming conflict with the standards of right and wrong which we accept for our private lives.

Most of us never seem to question the existence or the validity of such a double moral standard. Acts immoral within private moral judgment become sanctified if done in the name of the state by sometime armed with its authority.

The Notion of Expediency. It is within this relativist and (by private standards) amoral situation that the political notion of expediency is applicable. The idea means in practice that a state should always select and act upon that particular policy which is most likely to advance its interest in the given context. The only constant is national interest; all else is relative to the situation. Great decision and small alike are made in the light of this principle.

The most pressing question of our age—whether or not there is to be a total war which might well wipe out our civilization—will be in the last analysis answered according to the same general criteria that would determine whether or not a state should ratify a proposed treaty for the regulation of cod fishing.

We already know that in the process of selecting the most expedient from all the possible courses of action, a statesman always balances the advantages to be gained from any particular policy against the possible disadvantages arising from any certain or expected opposition by other states.

War, for example, becomes expedient when two factors are present simultaneously in the situation facing a state: (1) an objective which is sufficiently important to justify the risks and inescapable destruction of combat and which cannot be attained by any lesser means; (2) a power advantage which offers a sufficiently strong likelihood of winning the military test and of gaining the objective.

If both factors are present, a statesman can confidently accept war as a policy technique; if either is absent, war is inexpedient and probably will not be resorted to. All alternatives of policy are analyzed in the same way: the statesman 'balances of desirability of the possible with the possibility of the desirable' and strikes the best practicable compromise between them.

Two elements of the foregoing discussion require some further consideration. The first is the influence of situational factors in any policy decision; the second is the critical importance of maintaining the maximum number of alternatives of policy.

Although every state seeks to follow the dictates of national interest and designs a policy to chart a consistent course toward its objectives, these permanent and relatively fixed 'principles' of policy exercise only a partial control over the actual manoeuvring of the state.

Circumstances affect the conduct of international politics more than is often realized. The long-range policy of any government is subject to a constant buffeting of conditions which force major modifications. Among these can be included the action of other states, unexpected historical 'accidents,' and the impact of domestic policies.

As a statesman seeks to advance national interest in the face of all the rapidly changing circumstances he deals with, he has no other guide but expediency. He must be willing temporarily to abandon a long-range policy in order to seize a short-run gain, if such be the true course of expediency; on the other hand, he must not be overlay short-sighted in analyzing the expedient, or else he runs the danger of doing permanent injury to long-range national interest in the pursuit of the immediate.

Always, however, he finds that the formalized policy statements of his government provide an insufficient guide to action; he must be ever alert to recognise the extent and the form of the influence which conditions exert upon his policy.

A good illustration of this problem is provided by the course of American policy toward Yugoslavia since 1945, the United States attitude toward the government of Marshal Tito was controlled by the general policy principal of opposition to the dogma of communism and to its visible manifestation, the Soviet sphere of influence.

In 1948, there occurred the first break in the monolithic structure of the Soviet world; the expulsion of Tito from the councils of the communist elect.

Here was a circumstance that made much of our former policy obsolescent. No longer was it possible to consider communist ideology and the Soviet empire as being synonymous or coterminus. We were obliged to choose our real enemy from between the two in order to frame a policy that would be in harmony with the circumstances.

If we were primarily interested in fighting communist doctrine we should then attempt to destroy Tito's regime, which, alone and friendless, would have proved no formidable obstacle; if our true enemy was really Russian national power and imperialist policy, our course would then be to ally ourselves with Tito on the ground of identity of interest and thus to gain added strength for the bloc of which we were the leaders.

We chose the second course. All Americans know that national interest dictated our policy of cooperation with Yugoslavia which dates from our decision at that time. Such a policy is greatly at variance with our former doctrine of ideological purity.

It was not a happy choice that was forced upon us; many Americans are yet restive in any close relationship with a communist dictatorship, even an anti-Russian one.

Concept of Equilibrium

Dynamic Equilibrium. Although the dynamism of world affairs is apparent, it is not so immediately clear that they are constantly tending toward equilibrium. This point—a great cause for encouragement about the ultimate prospects of man—requires some analysis at this time.

So powerful are the forces of movement and change that this equilibrium can never, under our present system or organization, become static and permanent. A `dynamic equilibrium' in international relationships, however, not only is possible but is frequently attained.

This condition of relative balance between states is the principal means by which the world is spared the scourge of war in most crisis situations. Even when it exists, much change and modification in the relationships of states continues to take place.

The trend toward equilibrium usually confines the movement within the limits of safety, however, and non-violent resolutions are worked out for the problems that come up during the period of its effectiveness. Equilibrium breaks down and war comes only when the dynamic forces become too strong to be any longer confined.

Relations between any two states and within the system of states take place within a broad range relaxation to tension. Measures appropriate to a happy state of affairs are out of place in a time of tension, while extreme measures (violence and war) become practicable only in situations of great crisis.

In other words, if the state mechanism possessed the ability to prevent international crisis from passing the danger point of tension, the inclination to resort to violence would be lacking and greater reliance would instead be placed more orderly procedures.

Confinement of international politics within 'safe' limits would deliver man from at least the worst consequences of his inability to organize society upon a supra-national basis.

Although in no sense an automatic mechanism and of no guaranteed efficacy—failures have been many—factors do exist in world affairs which frequently serve as confining elements to state action in a crisis. The closer the world drifts toward war in the course of an international dispute, the greater the number of factors that appear to seek to halt the trend.

Perhaps, the most influential factors supporting this thesis are growing hazards of war for all states and the decreasing possibility of meaningful victory for any.

Techniques. Several techniques for bringing about equilibrium have been developed by diplomats in earlier eras and are being applied today.

The device of the sphere of influence, by means of which competing states mark off their respective areas of hegemony and each guarantees to respect the other's prior rights, repeatedly has proved capable of ending disputes and is today governing great-power relations in such territories as the Balkans.

The technique of the buffer zone also has had a great effect in restoring and preserving equilibrium by separating contending states by a neutral zone. Revival of this idea in the present day was indicated by the numerous proposals (mainly by Russia and France) looking toward a permanently neutralized Germany which made during 1954 and 1955.

Collective security, discussed briefly earlier and in more details below, may also be considered as a technique of equilibrium.

Perhaps the most elaborate system for the creation and maintenance of dynamic equilibrium is the balance of power. This idea is also considered in detail later in this chapter, but at this time we may point out its essential characteristic: an attempt to capitalize upon the inherent dynamism of world politics by creating a self-neutralizing situation. How this is done we shall see later.

Factors. Why is it becoming easier for the crises of world politics to be neutralized short of breakdown? Why are the factors making for equilibrium growth steadily stronger? To answer these questions fully would necessitate retelling the diplomatic history the past fifty years but some few general reasons may be suggested.

(1) The growing reluctance of states to resort of war. This subject is considered in the next section, but it may be said here that evidence is plentiful that states today are much less willing to accept war than they formerly were. This circumstance gives the neutralizing forces greater opportunity to do their work.

(2) The difficulty of isolating and confining war if it should occur. War, under contemporary technological conditions is tremendously contagious, and no state can be unconcerned about an outbreak war anywhere in the world. The best way for a state to void being drawn into a war in which it has little real interest is to help prevent that war from ever starting.

(3) The growing unwillingness of individuals to undergo the hardships of war for any but the most important of reasons. States passively endure provocations today that

would have been unbearable a few years ago because statesmen feel that they cannot ask their people to die for any but the most vital of interests.

(4) The increase in the number of expedient alternatives to war. As these continue to expand their area of effectiveness, more and more of interstate relations is coming within their scope. War becomes a less attractive means of accomplishing national purposes when there exist several other devices that offer promise of attaining the objective without the stresses and disruptions required by war.

Avoidance of War

War is generally admitted today, by statesmen and laymen alike, to be a course of last resort adopted only in desperate situations permitting of no other remedy. There is little moral revulsion in this evolving attitude, little idea that war is inherently wrong and evil. Instead it is, as are most of the decisions of statesmen, grounded primarily in considerations of practically and expediency.

Nevertheless, the growing reluctance of states to go to war is in itself a factor of stability which serves to make international politics somewhat less dangerous and unpredictable.

The Inexpediency of War. War is daily growing more inexpedient for most states. We saw above that war is selected as a technique of policy by states if two factors are present: an objective worthy of the efforts, and a reasonable probability of victory. On both counts war is today becoming less attractive.

Modern war is incredibly destructive. Modern 'total' weapons, with entire civilizations as their targets, are capable of wreaking great havoc upon any state in the world. In addition to the physical damage that war brings, organizing a nation to fight today involves a wholesale disruption and uprooting of the entire structure of social and economic life.

Even a state which, like the United States, escaped the physical destruction of World War II, suffered a great social and economic upheaval whose effects will continue to be felt for generations to come.

From the point of view both of the probable destruction and of the certain social and economic upset, war necessitates: tremendous effort on the part of any government and its people.

The Difficulty of Victory. A further factor makes war less expedient: the diminishing possibility of meaningful victory. Modern weapons are offensive weapons, and the best defence against them is the capacity for immediate reprisal. Thus, any statesmen calculating the desirability of war must gamble upon the possibility of a quick victory to end the struggle before it settles down to a grim process of mutual pulverization.

To gain this quick triumph requires an overwhelming preponderance of power. In early days when the outcome of a military defeat was merely a loss of territory to risk war upon nothing more substantial than a fairly good prospect of victory.

Today, when the penalty for losing a war may be national obliteration, this margin of advantage is insufficient. Great Superiority is necessary and, at least among the major states, it is a near impossibility to achieve.

Even the two great powers whose bitter controversy has earned the name of the 'cold war,' the United States and the Soviet Union, have been scrupulous not to present each other with ultimatums that might leave only the alternatives of capitulation or war.

Avoiding War by Compromise. Statesmen seek to avoid by compromising disputes upon the basis of relative involvements of interest and power. A given object of controversy may be a matter of deep interest to any party and of only minor concern to the other. If the relative involvements can be diplomatically determined and if the objective is one permitting such a technique of disposal, a compromise reflecting the differences in commitment is often not too difficult to arrange.

In theory this process would make wars forever obsolete. If power judgments could be made in an atmosphere of perfect rationality, statesmen could conduct their affairs like chess players. Calmly and soberly they would analyze their relative positions and power dispositions, foresee the inevitable end of the struggle, and either claim victory or accept defeat without any necessity of fighting the war at all.

Such detached objectivity is more than most statesmen are capable of, however, in the hectic atmosphere of international and domestic politics. It must also be admitted that the rigidity of the two-power world after 1945 made the diplomatic compromise a much less effective substitute for war than it might otherwise have been.

Avoiding War through Institutional Alternatives. A second basis for avoiding war is the settlement of disputes by an institutional instrument of some sort, the best known of which is the United Nations. The institutional approach to the avoidance of war has not prospered in the post-1945 era, and at present time it is of limited applicability.

Nevertheless, if most of mankind has its way, the day will come when the United Nations or some similar organization will be given effective power to enforce the rules of peaceful settlement. Today, with war growing daily less expedient, the long-range possibility of such a development is brighter than at any time in the past.

The Bases for Accepting War. Perhaps it is not too much to say that no war is inevitable. Somewhere along the chain of events that precede on outbreak of hostilities, one of the statesmen involved must make the critical choice. Should he select a different policy alternative, war over that issue can be avoided. Perhaps, the choice is made unknowingly; the fact remains, however, that in the course of every dispute there is a 'point of no return'.

Once the final step is taken, there is no way out but war. Realizing this fact, most policy makers was ever more warily as they near the point of the irrevocable decision.

A statesman chooses to resort to war in one of three circumstances: when he is under pressure from an inflamed national opinion which reckons not with possible defeat or rational goals of victory; when he recognises a threat to his state's vital interests that is so intimately bound up with national existence that in its defence the people would fight even a doomed war; or when he calculates that war in any particular situation is expedient.

Miscalculating the expediency of war is one of the most common dangers to peace. Once a leader decides that his power situation is such that he can safely risk a war, he tends to commit his state so deeply as to make withdrawal impossible if it should later become clear that he has made a mistake.

It must be kept in mind that in any dispute war may be inexpedient for both parties, or for either one; it cannot be expedient for both. Unless deprived of free choice by some irrational force, a state in a condition of actual power inferiority to its opponent does not accept war unless it is unaware or unconvinced of its weakness.

In modern world politics, such miscalculation often brings complete disaster. One need look no further than the consequences of Germany's misjudgments of Great Britain in 1914, of the United States in 1917, and of Great Britain again in 1939 and 1940 to find corroborating evidence.

Communist leadership also apparently miscalculated United States reaction in 1950 at the time of the commencement of the war in Korea. In all of these cases, war originally thought expedient proved not to be so because of an analytical error.

Contemporary Techniques for Avoiding War. The present structure of world politics affords several interesting examples of the techniques employed by states to avoid war. Remembering that modern war, to be practical, must involve a great power superiority over any enemy, every state has sought to escape from positions of inferiority to any probable foe. In doing so, most of them have fled to the protection of the great blocs led by the United States and the Soviet Union.

These massive alliances confront each other today in a state of baffled hostility. Exactly how much each alliance has contributed to the strength of the United States and the USSR as regards each other is open to question; certainly neither has won any great victories over the other since the alliances came into being.

It is neither clear that within at least the Western alliance there is much working at cross purposes. American policy makers have viewed their group as added support for United States policy in the cold war against the Soviet Union and have assumed that our allies are motivated by the same purposes as we have been.

On the other hand, many of the associates of the United States joined the group as a means of reducing the possibility of their being drawn into a war, and they would consider a war begun by the United States and serving American national interest as being just as undesirable as one begun by the Russians. As a result, there is a constant controversy going on within the Western bloc.

Mere recently this concern with their own vulnerability has led some of the smaller states to join a new grouping led by India. This bloc has not formalized its status by written agreement, but its over-all position is clear. It rejects both alliances as being equally war-minded and is establishing for itself a position of neutrality and mediation between them.

In this effort the Indian (sometimes called 'Arab-Asian') bloc seems to have gained some support from many people now included in one of the bipolar groupings. For example, in the debates in the United Nations during August 1953 dealing with the details of the final truce in Korea and the proposed political conference to be held there, several allies of the United States, including Australia and the Philippines, deserted the American position to side with India.

The neutral bloc's position grew more strategic as the cold war relaxed during 1954 and 1955. All this manoeuvring has its root a desire on the part of each of the weaker states not to be caught in a position of such weakness as to make war upon it expedient on the part of a stronger neighbour.

The Development of Institutions

A final technique of stability in international politics remains to be considered. This is the development of international institutions. Although we know already that the institutional structure of interstate life is incomplete and of limited effectiveness, formalized institutions are nevertheless significant in themselves and of great importance as possible harbingers of the future.

The present generation is not the first to discover that international politics is logically anarchic and provocative of tension and crisis. The student is struck by the long history of man's attempts to discover a route of escape from this condition. One of the principal methods employed has been the deliberate creation of new international institutions and the strengthening of existing ones. These institutions have developed by drawing analogies with private civil life.

In highly organized private society, the institutions that surround us are constructed upon unpredictable behaviour patterns of individuals. We know, for example, that private citizens will not normally settle their disputes by violence but will have recourse to the courts.

This tends to make interpersonal relations more orderly and stable and provides a greater measure of personal security. Indeed, without the institutional framework ordering individual relationships, social life would be nearly impossible to endure.

If some such institutional framework were to be created for control of sovereign states, much of the anarchy of international life would be eliminated. Therefore, international institutions seek to prohibit certain modes of alternative procedures for the satisfaction of the legitimate desires of states.

Up to now, their impact upon world politics has been peripheral; if they should succeed in materially increasing their scope, the shape and texture of interstate relations would be improved.

The Institutions of International Life. The analysis of the institutions of the world political community will be undertaken in later chapters. At this point we need only name and briefly characterize the more important of them.

International law is a body of rules and principles that specify the rights of states and lay down the procedures to be followed by states in dealing with each other. It includes mechanism for the settlement of interstate disputes upon the basis of legal right as well as techniques for the redress of injury. Much of international relations is already within its scope, and the attempt to enlarge its area of effectiveness is a continuous one.

International organization is the term applies to permanent associations of sovereign states which have become sufficiently formalized to acquire an international status. The United Nations is one with a generalized multi-purpose mission; hundreds exist with more specialized purposes.

Through these organizations states develop regularized procedures for co-operative action, and in the aggregate a remarkably large proportion of international contact takes place within the institutional structure.

The third international institution that merits our attention is supra-national government. Only in the present generation has this concept transcended mere abstract speculation and entered the stage of significant development. It involves the partial merging of the sovereignties of the member states to create new instruments of government with real, though limited, power.

For the special purposes of the organization, the participating states forswear their sovereign independence and full authority is exerted by the new authority. Of the many proposals for such organizations made since World War II, by the end of 1955 only the European Coal and Steel Community had entered upon its operations, but its success and the logic of its organization promised and several others would come into early existence.

Organizing and Operating Concepts

In the preceding section we considered the techniques employed by statesmen to enable them to accomplish their mission within the requirements of the state system. We now turn to an analysis of a somewhat more formalized development of the same general idea: the various concepts that seek to provide general organizing and operating hypotheses for the entire structure of international politics.

These all seek to bring a higher degree of order and predictability into the international relationships by establishing single principles upon which to base all political action. Each of them is dynamic, in the sense that it accepts the inevitability of change in interstate life.

Each has at one time or another been asserted to be the single route to stability and peace that the world must follow; each has had its more or less successful application at particular periods of history, and each has undergone its periods of ineffectiveness and failure.

We shall examine four of them in some detail; the concept of the great powers, the concept of the concert of power, the concept of balance of power, and the concept of collective security. They all share a common preoccupation with the phenomenon of power and the need for its control each attempts the solution of the problem in a different way.

The Great Power Concept

The Role of the Great Power. The first principle is the idea of the great powers. It owes its origin to a factor mentioned in Chapters 2 and 4; despite the legal equally which states pretend to enjoy, there are actually wide variations in their power and thus in their relative ability to achieve their ends. One group of states that individually encompass great concentrations of power and collectively dominates world politics has come to be called the 'great powers.'

Historically, the shape of world affairs has been determined by the relations of the great power to each other. The present pattern of international relations has been laid down by these few states simply because they have had available the power to support pretensions to superior status.

The great powers have determined the standards of international conduct; they have asserted the right to be consulted upon any question in which they have taken an interest; they have created world-wide empires; they have repeatedly redrawn the map of the world; they alone have been able to force the entire world to go to war.

Their superior position has enabled them to concentrate their attention upon their relations with one another, dealing with small states by means of consideration of status and prestige instead of by raw power.

Such has been their dominant position that most smaller states have found it impossible to remain aloof from great-power politics. The majority have found it expedient to attach themselves at one time or another to the protection of one of the great powers upon the latter terms, and then to work out their further policy within this framework.

The Group of Great Powers. The number of great powers has varied from time to time but has always been relatively small. During most of the nineteenth century all of them were European. Austria, Prussia, Great Britain, and Russian were the 'Big Four' of the Congress of Vienna in 1815, joined shortly thereafter by France as the Napoleonic issue diminished in importance.

Later in the century Italy was accepted as an additional member and Gemany replaced. Prussia. Around the 1900 the European monopoly upon great power status was broken with the maturing of the United States and Japan. World War I was resulted in Austria-Hungary's disappearance from the group and the temporary eclipse of Russia and Germany.

World War II shook up the memberships seriously and it has not again stabilized. Japan and Germany were crushed temporarily and the terms of their acceptance have not yet been decided; Italy and France were so badly injured that their return to full status in the group at any time in the future is most doubtful; Great Britain was grievously weakened and has been so far unable to meet all the requirements of a great power.

The United States and the Soviet Union emerged from the war as the only survivors of the old group. Indeed, their power position was improved not only relatively but absolutely; so great was their margin of superiority that a new term was coined and some called them the "super-powers."

Today the United States and the USSR still dominate the scene; Great Britain, Germany, France, and Japan are hoping to recapture former eminence while two new aspirants for memberships, China and India, are seeking to qualify.

The Decline of the Great Power Concept The great-power principle—that only the great powers matter and that their decisions are binding upon all states—has been to a great degree weakened by the rise of nationalism. The upsurge of national spirit in the smaller states has given rise on their part to a reluctance and a great resistance to being taken for granted.

Populations of smaller states, especially those that have only recently won their independence feel that their national objections and aspirations are just as valid and worthy of consideration as those of the people of a great war. In order to escape from great-power domination and to devise means to make their independence effective, small states often concert together.

One of their favourite techniques in recent years has involved the use of the mechanism of international organization. Much of the history of both the League of Nations and the United Nations can be told in terms of the more or less successful attempt of the small states to avoid being mere pawns of the great powers.

For half a century the most eloquent spokesmen for the philosophy of international organization have come from the ranks of the lesser powers; contemporary figures include Herbert Evatt of Australia, Carlos Romulo of the Philippines, Paul-Henri Speak of Belgium, Sir Leslie Munro of New Zealand, and Tryge Lie of Norway, the first Secretary-General of the United Nations.

The great-power principle has been seriously compromised by this outbreak of resentment and resistance among the citizens of the lesser powers, and no longer can it be successfully argued that only the foreign policies of the handful of great states are of real importance.

Small states, either through the identity of their policies with mass opinion through the world or through their total power when they combine forces, represent points of view which the great powers watch carefully and take due account of.

This may be portent of a fundamental change in the character of world policies, or it may be only temporary loss of position by the great powers. It is beyond doubt, however, that the principle of the great powers today has little relevance to the current world situation. The remainder of the world would simply refuse to be disposed of by any small group of states.

The Concept of the Concert of Power

A second concept of organization is the concert of power. The idea received its greatest formulation at the time of the Congress of Vienna in 1815, although it is actually much older, but briefly, the notion has at its root the idea of the privileged role of the great powers and goes on from there to postulate that these few states have the right and the duty of concert together and to arrange all international affairs to suit their common convenience. It may be thought of as a techniques for making the principle of the great power more effective.

Historical Incidence. During the period of reaction in Europe which followed the final victory over Napoleon in 1815, the concert of power sought to suppress the bogey of revolution wherever it might appear. The leading members of the concert were Austria, Russia and Prussia; France was a later adherent and Britain an irregular participant. Under the leadership and guidance of Austria, the major states held several formal conferences to deal with specific revolutionary crises and in between maintained close contact with each other.

Throughout the remainder of the nineteenth century the concert, including all the European great powers, functioned fitfully; effectively in 1856, 1878 and 1905 and unsuccessfully in 1827, 1848, and 1870. The final failure was its greatest; it proved unable to ward off war in 1914.

In disrepute during the interwar period, the principle was made respectable again during World War II. The various 'Big Three' and 'Big Four' conference at which Roosevelt, Churchill, Stalin, and other leaders shaped joint strategy represented a renewal of the old idea.

The privileged position given permanent members of the Security Council of the United Nations is another example of the contemporary validity of the concept; under the charter and the rule of great-power unanimity in the security council (the 'veto') the major states collectively exercise a virtual monopoly over questions involving the maintenance of peace.

Strengths and Weaknesses of the Concert. It cannot be doubted that at particular moments the concert of power has proved to be most effective in preserving or restoring international peace. It is nevertheless painfully clear that the concert has failed in as spectacular a fashion on other occasions, and that its current manifestations, either in the security council or in the 'Big Four', have proved unable to end the long crisis that grips the contemporary world.

The reasons for the dramatic successes of the concert principles and its equally dramatic failures and found in the basic assumptions upon which the whole idea is grounded. There must be substantial agreement among the members of the concert—or at least among the preponderant majority of them—upon a general line of policy before the concert technique can produce significant results.

This is why the concert is most effective in protecting the *Status quo.* When the members of the concert are satiated and have a common interest in the perpetuation of what is for them a desirable arrangement, they can easily unite to subdue any potential upsetting force as being equally a threat to all of them.

When there is no consensus upon the desirability of the *status quo* but instead a sizable proportion of the great powers is more interested in altering the distribution of rewards, then the concert cannot succeed.

It breaks down when revisionist states are powerful and united enough to make the risk of breaking the peace worth taking. In other works, the agreement underlying an effective application of the concert of power is not different from any other type of international agreement. It comes into being as result of an identity of interest among states and endures only so long as the interests coincide.

It seems obvious that the concept of the concert is of only remote significance in the world today. Because the type of situation in which it is most effective does not exist. The great powers today do not share an `area of agreement' regarding the over-all structure of world politics and thus the essential precondition to an effective concert is lacking.

Before the principle can again become effective, an identity of interest must develop not only between the United States and the Soviet Union but also among all the other states that qualify as great powers.

Although great-power discussions were begun again in 1955, it is scarcely overpessimistic to predict that the full-fledged revival of the concert is still long way in the future.

The Balance of Power

General Theory: The principle of the balance of power is somewhat better known than are the first two. It has as its ideal a state of international equilibrium arrived at not only by confining relationships into a set pattern but by accepting the dynamism of world politics and utilizing them to secure peace. It enjoys one great advantage over the concert.

The later usually necessitates basic agreement among participating states in order to operates; the balance instead can function in a situation of conflict and disagreement. This makes the balance applicable in a somewhat broader variety of circumstances.

The balance has at its centre an idea to which we have earlier alluded; a statesman will not normally resort to war when the odds are heavily against him. In operation, the balance of power is supposed to arrange matter so that any state which seeks to upset the peace will automatically have ranged against it sufficient powers to persuade it of the folly.

Prerequisites: Dispersal and Fluidity. To be effective, the balance mechanism requires a relatively wide distribution of power among the states of the world. It is self-evident that when a single state or a small group of states enjoys a near hegemony, a much greater temptation exists on their part to attempt adventuresome policies backed by a willingness to go to war.

Only when power is widely dispersed can the peace be preserved by the balance because only then is the international situation sufficiently fluid to permit states to move with the requisite freedom.

The regulatory mechanism of the balance of power therefore cannot be effective unless international alignments are flexible and states are comparatively free to select the most expedient course in each situation as it arises. Concentrations of power and rigidity of relationships are the twin phenomena which the advocates of the balance recognize as the greatest dangers to peace. Accordingly, dispersal and fluidity are regarded as indispensable prerequisites for its operation.

Prerequisite: The Holder of the Balance: Most states are concerned lest they be menaced by superior power and therefore do what they can in the interest of guaranteeing its effective distribution. It can thus be argued that all states employ the balance principle in framing their policies. Upon a wide basis, however, the concept is significant only when a single state or bloc of states makes the preservation of the balance the major component of its policy.

The "bolder of the balances" must be relatively powerful in its own right and have the preservation of peace as a matter of fundamental national interest. It must therefore be a highly satiated power with a vested interest in the *status quo.* If it meets the requirements and plays its part with resolution and firmness. It can be the key to the entire international situation.

An essential in a state's manipulation of the balance is the freedom of action it is able to exercise; in preserving international fluidity it must always guarantee itself the maximum practical number of alternative courses of action. In practice this requires that, in so far as possible.

Such a state avoid bidding commitments to others and that it be prepared to rid itself of any become unduly restrictive. The balancing power must therefore eschew my obsessive moralistic or legalistic concern in its policy, since these tend to impose a rigidity of thought and action that is fatal to the policy of the balance.

Diplomatic following the strategy of the balance must be extremely skilful, have a clear idea of the requirements of such a policy, and possess the courage to make unpopular decisions.

The Balance Principle in Operation. If the international situation is appropriately fluid, the holder of the balance can move with some confidence. Relieved of major commitments or absolute objectives, it is free to preserve the condition of dispersed power and to impede the creation of hard-and-fast alignments tending toward dangerous concentrations of power.

An impeding crisis calls for the holder of the balance to move with determination. As the linen of the dispute harden the balancing state decides which of the disputing parties (if either of them) is willing to carry the dispute to the point of war. In practice this is usually the stronger party, since only for it would war be expedient.

The holder of the balance then places itself unreservedly and promptly in support of the peaceful side and thus presents the potential warm maker with the practical alternatives of military defeat or the abandonment of its aggressive policy. If the peaceful side becomes bellicose in its turn as a result of the increased strength arising from the balancer's support, the latter must be prepared to shift its allegiance to the original aggressor, and continue its move back and forth until both are convinced that any war started by either of them would have to be fought against superior force. Once the crisis passes, the balancing state resumes its independent role until new situation arises to call it into action again as a peacemaker.

Britain and the Balance. The balance of power is generally identified with the name of Great Britain. During several centuries Britain diplomacy self-consciously sought to create situations favourable to British exercise of the role of holder of the balance.

Its success was considerable, and British experience is most instructive to any state aspiring to follow its example. European peace was the dominate Britain interest (desirable to enable Britain to concentrate its attention upon its overseas empire).

In pursuing the strategy of the balance, the British attempted to avoid being drawn into binding arrangements with any European power which might prove restriction. Britain policy minimized moral absolutes and concentrated upon a realistic version of national interests.

Britain therefore systematically obstructed any policy aimed at domination of the European continent by any state. Despite its lack of moral or legal justification, the balance principle under British direction succeeded in creating and maintaining one of the longest periods of comparative peace in world history.

The balance failed to head off World War I, because the necessary conditions for its success no longer obtained; the lines of alliance in Europe had become rigid, and British strength had become dissipated to the point where its joining the Entente in 1912 made little difference. The scales were not so decisively tripped by British action that the Central Powers would call off the war.

Between World War I and World War II, Britain made some attempts to renew its policy of the balance, but the serious worsening in its power position ultimately persuaded its leaders to seek to appease to dictators. After 1945, Britain sought again for a brief period to hold the balance between the United States and the Soviet Union.

Unable to maintain the requisite independent policy, the British government soon recognized the futility of any such programme. Today Britain is in no position to play its traditional role, although much of its present policy (for example, its relative reluctance to join in the movement for European unification) undoubtedly looks forward to the way when conditions will be again favourable fcr a renewal of the role of holder of the balance.

The Balance in the Future. There is a body of informed opinion in the United States today that contents that only the reapplication of the balance principle can the stalemate of contemporary world politics be broken. If by that they mean that the United States should recognize the dangers inherent in any over-concentration of national power and should work to break up any such concentration, and that Americans should not allow concern such private morality to obscure the national interest, it is impossible to disagree with them.

If, however, these evangels of the balance are proposing that the United States take upon itself the free-wheeling course followed by Great Britain during the previous century, there is little that can be said in their defence.

The United States could not become the holder of the balance without breaking nearly all its binding commitments and assuming a role close to that of our nineteenth-century isolation. This is a policy whose outcome would be perilous in the extreme. Furthermore, no matter how willing the United States might be to manipulate the balance, it would be a hopeless to attempt to do so until the rigidity of the two-power world has been further relaxed.

The balance is a dynamic concept that draws its strength from movement, and so long as the two giants keep the world locked up in a great armed camps, the freedom of choice which the principle demands simply does not exist.

The two-power world may be in a process of break-up, as some qualified observers feel; even so the United States could not assume the role of the holder without sacrificing its place as leader of the free world. This last alternatives is one which many observers are not yet ready to advocate.

If the two-power world no longer existed and the situation were again ripe for the application of the balance principle, it is probable that some other power or power bloc than the United States would emerge as holder of the balance. American commitments are too widely dispersed and our involvements are too deep to permit us to free ourselves without causing chaos.

India and its allies constitute a strong candidate for the future balancer; the Indian policy of avoiding fixed arrangements with either camp and the demarcation of distinct third position between them gives clear evidence that the Indian government is thinking in these terms.

Another conceivable nominee is China, if it could free itself from Russian control; so is united Europe after the current trends toward consolidation have reached sufficient maturity.

It is possible to entertain a cautions optimism about the future of the balance principle. Obviously it remain an academic concern so long as the only ponderables on the international scene are the Russian bloc and the American bloc.

It is self-evident, that the smaller states are growing increasingly restive under their manipulation by the great antagonists, and that resentment is now beginning to be reflected in concrete policy.

If the Afro-Asian-Arab bloc led by India continues to gain strength, cohension, and new recruits from the other camps, the possibility exists that it might be able, on a limited scale, to hold the balance between the United States and the USSR

In that way the new group might keep the two alliance from one another's throat long enough to permit irritated nationalism to cool and the adjustments of policy to take place which are necessary for continued co-existence. If the balance principle could neutralize the most dangerous aspects of the cold war, it would more than justify the most extravagnza claims made in its behalf.

Collective Security

We know already that as a scheme it involves primarily two components, the exchange of security guarantees by all participating states, through which the security of any is protected by all, and the creation of mechanisms to make these guarantees effective.

Many proposals have been advanced to implement the idea, their number and the rapidity with which they have been suggested increasing in recent years as war has grown more dangerous for all states.

In the present day, the idea of collective security continues to exercise a great attraction of statesmen and private individuals alike, as new weapons, tactical theories, and techniques for warfare make an outbreak of war progressively more frightening prospect.

For collective security to be an effective base for international action, two requirements must be satisfied.

In the first place, there must be general acceptance on the part of all states involved that the maintenance of peace is a vital interest. In other worlds, none must be pursuing an objective of such great importance that it is willing to go to war over it.

All must be willing to accept non-violent solutions in such conflicts of interest as arise among them.

Generally speaking, a state may be brought to the recognition of the critical importance of the maintenance of peace for either of two reasons: either the state is generally satiated and hence is willing to forswear further military adventures, or else the state is in such a vulnerable position that, despite the urgent promptings of national interest, to seek to accomplish its ends by war might prove fatal. In today's world, it is not too much to say that all states fall into one or another of these categories, with many more in the second than in the first. Many governments, however, have not recognized this.

The second requirement for successful collective security is the existence of acceptable alternative procedures to substitute for war. Any system is founded upon the sovereign state must provide outlets for the dynamism of interstate relations and failure to do so makes the search for peace fruitless.

Stability in international politics cannot be reached by attempts to freeze the relations between states; it must take the form of the dynamic equilibrium we discussed earlier what collective security seeks to accomplish is to insure that inevitable change takes place peacefully.

Regional and General Systems. In theory, collective security in the true sense is applicable only to the entire state system, since only then would the peace it would bring be general. Up to the present time, however, general collective security has not been made into a reality. The principal defect in such essays as have been undertaken has been the failure to meet the first requirement mentioned above: the recognition of the maintenance of peace as the *summum bonum* of interstate life.

It is a peculiarity of collective security as an idea that peace is attainable only by being willing to fight for it, and both before and since World War II, many states have proved unable to grasp this notion.

Absolute peace necessitates total commitment of all states to preservation, and as soon as any considerable portion of the membership of the state system abstains from the mutual guarantee, the collective character of the idea disappears.

Under the League of Nations system and within the United Nations, many states have indicated that they did not and do not believe in the indivisibility of peace and in the necessity of taking joint action to prevent a successful aggression.

Passive disapproval of expansion by force, even when delivered with near unanimity, has proved to be insufficient to make collective security a reality. General agreement upon positive action is necessary.

Although collective security upon a general basis has been beyond attainment up to the present, much greater success has been obtained in the application of the principle to geographically limited areas.

In such arrangements, the participating states mutually guarantee each other's security, both as regards the members of the group and as regards outside states.

In addition, mechanism are usually provided by means of which alternative non-violent procedures are stipulated to govern the relationship between the members.

Perhaps the best known of the many recent examples of regional collective security arrangement is the North Atlantic Treaty (1949). In this document, the fifteen participating states first agree to settle all disputes arising among themselves by pacific means.

In later sections it is stipulated that an attack upon any one of the signatories would be deemed an attack upon all, and that all would thereupon concert together in order to decide upon and to take appropriate action. We can see that these two notions sum up the entire heart of the concept of collective security.

The Case of Korea. Perhaps the most impressive test to which collective security has been put up was the intervention of the United Nations into the fighting in Korea between 1950 and 1953. The reasons for military action on the part of the seventeen nations represented there involved both the collective concept of the maintenance of general peace (the necessity of punishing an aggressor) and their individual concern with self-defence.

In the first place, the unequal contributions made by the membership of the United Nations to what was declared to be a common operation shown the unequal extent to which the idea had taken hold. Some states saw in communist military aggression a threat to the fragile fabric of peace and reached promptly and with determination, others contributed only few forces and those grudgingly; still others remained aloof.

In the second place, the common military venture in Korea could not be interpreted as setting a definite precedent in the event similar situations arose in the future.

The United Nations decision to act was taken as promptly as it was only because of the accident of Soviet boycott of the Security Council during the summer of 1950; once returned, the USSR demonstrated its willingness to veto any further moves to implement the original directive. So long as the Soviet-Western split continues, general collective security through the United Nations will be limited in its application to those few points upon which East and West agree.

Thirdly, despite the foregoing criticisms, the Korean matter proved that collective security as a concept was workable and indeed a necessary idea if peace is to be the lot of mankind.

4

Conflict Area in World Politics

The world politics is characterized by movement and change. States pursue their policies in an active fashion, come into contact with other states doing the same thing, and readjust their relationships accordingly. Sometimes these contact reflect a coincidence of national interest and the ensuing relationship is harmonious and cooperative.

More frequently national interests disagree and there develops a situation of international conflict. This chapter makes an attempt to examine in detail the phenomenon of international conflict, the situations out of which it arises, and the techniques of conflict used by states.

International conflict is an inevitable feature of world politics. Although it is too much to say that conflict is perpetual, it recurs so frequently in international affairs as to make justifiable the claims that it is a thoroughly normal relationship between states. No state can hope to escape conflict with other states in the accomplishment of even its minimum policy objectives.

A Competitive System. The nation-state system is inherently and intensively competitive. States, insistent upon the universal recognition of their political independence and their freedom of choice and action, find themselves trapped by the converse of the proposition: they must grant every other state the same freedom and independence and hence cannot trust any one but themselves. They must seek salvation by their own efforts and maintain a suspicious and distrustful attitude toward every state with which they have relations.

Security can be absolute only when a state controls more power than the remainder of the world combined. Every state feels that this would be a desirable situation for itself; however, when any one takes a step, no matter how small, toward the attainment of this objective all other states feel less secure with connection to the one gaining strength. In this generally competitive situation conflict becomes inevitable. Any state, feeling itsel f a free agent, will oppose any other state that is following a course thought to be inimical to its interest.

A second factor tending toward conflict in international politics is the absolute character of so many objectives of national policy today. As we said earlier, a limited objective that is out in concrete terms is capable of achievement; an imprecise and absolute objective tends instead to involve the state seeking its continuous inconclusive struggle. The promotion of national ideology, the enhancement of national prestige, the augmentation of national power: these are absolute objectives that attract controversy because of their very lack of rational content and clearly defined limits.

Even such concrete objectives as territorial integrity and political independence have been on a occasion conceived in such absolute terms as to bring conflict in their train that would otherwise have been avoidable. The nation-state system, emphasizing the freedom of action of the individual state, is constructed in such a way as to make international conflict likely.

Policy conflicts reflecting disagreements of national interest are common enough, but another types of international conflict adds greatly to world tension. This is the struggle between embattled nationalism, a phenomenon of increasing familiarity.

Conflicts of interest usually have in their background some basis or rational and realistic calculation by statesmen; the same cannot be said for national controversy. By definition nationalism is an emotion and hence is irrational; its contribution to world politics has largely taken the form of reducing the rational content of policy.

Modern nationalism is no longer content with securing the political independence of the nation; in many societies it has acquired a missionary zeal to spread its message beyond the state's boundaries and to secure converts by persuasion and force. When two such expanding ideologies come into contact, no outcome is possible except an immediate bitter hostility. Nationalism is often an effective instrument used by statesmen in support of rationally determined policy, but it is not susceptible to being turned on and off as political conditions dictate. It persists in holding on to its emotional patterns of attachment and hate long after any rational reason for either emotion exists. Many states have become involved in conflicts with others with which they had no quarrel of interest merely because of the promotings of an outraged nationalism.

TYPES OF CONFLICT

Undoubtedly, no two international conflicts are same. Each participant brings to the struggle a different policy, power position, and degree of involvement and a state caught in a controversy today will go at it differently from the way it would have yesterday or would tomorrow. It is nevertheless possible it distinguish between the two major types or categories of international conflict upon the basis of the principal techniques relied upon by the disputing parties.

Violent conflict, the first type, involves the use of physical violence by each participating state as the primary means of accomplishing its policy objective; in non-violent conflict on the other hand, major reliance is placed upon other means.

Violent Conflict

War is the most common form of violent international conflict. War is a legal status as well as means of executing policy, but in the present connection we shall consider it only as a condition of international relations featured by the use of organized and unlimited violence as a means of securing agreement among states. War is an instrument of policy, used by states when it is appropriate from the point of view both the objective sought and of the strength of the prospective enemy. It is the ultimate form of settling disputes in international affairs and is the only means now available to obtain a final solution to an international problem.

Inevitability of War: In the literature of international politics no subject is more frequently debated than the inevitability of war. Many arguments are advanced to support the thesis that violent conflict is an inescapable part of interstate life; the combativeness of man, the competitive instinct the theory of evolution, the incompatibility of diverse cultures, and the sacredness of ideologies are only a few chosen at random from among the strong views on this subject.

Philosophers, such as Nietzsche, Sorel, and other apologists for Fascism, have conjured up the theory of what might be called 'therapeutic war'; they argue that 'war is the health of the state' and see in violent interstate conflict a desirable and elevating custom that raises civilization to its highest peak.

Who deny the inescapability of war, point to the progressive elimination of violence from human social life in other areas as proof that there is nothing immutable about the institution of international violence.

We may conclude that under the prevailing conditions of interstate life conflict is as close to an inevitability as anything human ever is; the system and the character of the participants combine to make disagreement as normal and much more common than agreement. But conflict is not synonymous with war; private citizens have their conflicts under a legal order without resorting to violence.

The decision whether or not to choose violence as the technique of international conflicts is usually a deliberate one, made by statesmen upon the basis of the particular situation and the position in which the state finds itself. Conflict itself is inevitable, but no particular war is inevitable.

Can War be Eliminated? Since the decision to make war is based upon the importance of the objective sought and the probability of victory, the logical route to the abolition of the institution would seem to lie through an attack upon the conditions that make war profitable.

If all the objectives in which behalf war is undertaken were attainable by non-violent means, or if these were no objectives worth while enough to justify violence, there would be no point in fighting.

These were substantially the arguments of the advocates of collective security and world government. If the legitimate desires of states were satisfied by peaceful and co-operative means, and an overwhelming preponderance of the states of the world guaranteed each other's security against a potential aggressor, violence in international affairs would disappear as completely as it has gone from private life.

Individuals in domestic affairs still occasionally run amok and make use of indiscriminate personal violence, it is true; society has created means of coping with them, however, administering punishment for their violation of the social rules. There also would remain the possibility in a world government of any resort to violence; it would be the responsibility of the group to device techniques of control and punishment for this form of antisocial behaviour. Thus, even the disciples of world government cannot and do not guarantee: completely non-violent system of international relations, even if their proposal should adopted.

The best summary view of the inevitability of international violence seems to be that war is not truly inevitable, but that under present conditions of international life it is an omnipresent possibility and sometimes an over powering probability.

Causes of International Violence. War is, as Clausewitz's classic phrase has it, 'the continuation of policy by other means.' The object of any policy is the attainment of the objective sought, and war as a policy technique must be measured in terms of its effectiveness in gaining the real objectives of the state.

The first cause of war is always some form of international

disagreement and the reason war is undertaken is to secure the compliance of the enemy. This means that any war worth the effort must be in the service of an attainable set of on objects.

It is particularly apposite in regard to such risky and destructive business as modern war. If a war is undertaken without any clear idea of what will be done with victory, even glorious success on the battlefield becomes a hollow triumph when the final results are analyzed.

The violence of war should be proportional to the objective in view. The complete destruction of the enemy, however, satisfying to nationalist appetities, often redounds to a state's embarrassment. The question of Germany, for example, was not eliminated from international relations by the crushing defeat of the Nazis in 1945; on the contrary, Germany's former enemies have been required hastily to rebuild its power and to seek its assistance.

With the clarity of hindsight the free world understands today how much better it would have been to have applied only enough military pressure upon Germany to destroy the insanity of Hitler and then to welcome back a strong but free Germany into the body of nations. Instead we created the power vacuum in central Europe that has proved to be so troublesome.

One example is furnished by the course of the Korean struggle after 1950. Part of the uncertainty that gripped United Nations leadership throughout 1951 and 1952 arose from a widely held conviction that a military victory there would not necessarily achieve the objectives sought in the first place.

To contradict a famous General, in war there is a substitute for military victory: the attainment of the political objectives for which the war was undertaken. Too much battlefield success may be as great an impediment to the attainment of a state's real interest as too little.

Limited War. Such struggle is fought for precise and well-understood objectives by both sides; the violence used is controlled as strictly as pòssible, with only those measures being taken that contribute directly to the attainment of the objectives of the belligerents; the war is broken off at the moment the objectives are attained or when either party realizes that further struggle is useless because the objective is unattainable; and the conclusion of peace is followed by the restoration of normal relations between the former enemies.

Limited war is not necessarily mild or restrained; it may be extremely destructive and bloody. What makes it distinctive, however is that destruction and bloodshed are undertaken not for their own sakes but only after deliberate decision that such measures are necessary to the accomplishment of the political objective.

The most familiar illustration of the efficacy of the technique of limited war is the series of wars undertaken by Prince Bismarck in the nineteenth century while he was engaged in the process of creating a unified Germany. The Danish War of 1864, the Austrian War of 1866, and are French War of 1870-71 were all necessary steps in his programme of erecting a single German government.

Total War. The improvements in the technology of warfare and the increasing demands of nationalist hysteria have given war a new outlook in the modern times. At least as far as major powers are concerned, limited war as just discussed has been largely replaced by a new concept, ' total' war. Technologically it is no longer possible to apply violence with near surgical precision; new weapons and techniques are those of mass destruction and are particularly applicable to civilian populations.

In such a situation statesmen are required to invoke the most extreme nationalist reactions from their people in order to gain the necessary high degree of commitment from all individuals, and super-patriotism and bitter hatred of the enemy become the normal order of the day in a state engaged in a total war.

Thus technology and nationalism join forces to make this type of conflict: struggle of peoples against peoples. In this combat, no objectives are conceivable except total ones; nationalist attitudes are not satisfied with anything than the complete destruction of the enemy. His territory must be occupied, his government extinguished, his ideology repudiated, and his state and remade in the image of the victor. These objectives—irrational and imprecise—make any war likely to become a war of annihilation. If a government is losing a limited war it is good sense to give serious thought to calling an end to the struggle, since its leaders realize that peace would be made in terms of specific objectives and the defeated party would be allowed to continue its national existence.

In total war, defeat necessarily involves Since a government knows that to surrender places it completely at the enemy's mercy, there is no particular advantage to ending the struggle as long as any capacity to resist remains. Thus total war tends to require total victory.

New Weapons—the atomic and hydrogen bombs, guided missiles of tremendous destructiveness, supersonic aircraft, and so on—and the different psychology of warfare have created something of a revolution in strategy. No longer is the principal target of military power the armed forces of the enemy; since armies today are mere rabbles without ample supply and energetic high command, the enemy's productive machine and his political and social morale become objectives of primary concern. The atomic bomb is relatively ineffective against dispersed troops in the field, but has high efficiency when exploded in a crowded urban area. So it goes with other weapons; there is some doubt about the tactical worth of atomic artillery. So much will the enemy be concentrating upon the destruction of civilian society behind the lines that the combat soldier will be left in relative place. This jocular exaggeration conceals a profound truth. International conflict of the total war variety has many implications for every individual everywhere.

To take World War II as a fair example of a total war, there is much doubt about the efficacy of this technique in attaining national objectives. It is only under rare and extreme circumstances that any state's real national interest would be served by securing the complete destruction of another state, even if it were possible completely to wipe a modern state off the face of the earth.

Total war may yet revolutionize international relations, either by causing such havoc as to destroy modern civilization as by precipitating a popular revulsion against war by world public opinion that bring about effective world organization to prevent it. Statesmen generally realize the irrationality of total war. Charged at they are with the necessity of advancing the interest of their respective states, they cannot afford the luxury indulging in the nationalist excesses that are involved in the concept. But nationalist plays its part in even the most detached policy judgments, and the tendency to think in terms of a ' showdown' by force with a stubborn enemy is alway. present.

The great powers of the contemporary world tend to move quickly, if sometimes at cross purposes, to end the little wars that flare up between smaller states before rival nationalism get hold of them and begin to agitate for the struggle.

Non-Violent Conflict

Non-violent conflict includes the great bulk of international conflicts: those that do not reach the point of organized hostility and the employment of force. At the outset it must again be stressed that the only real difference between violent and non-violent conflict is one of techniques; in all other respects they are exactly similar.

Both grow out of the same types of situation, both are marked by the attempt of the participants to coerce the other into agreement with it, both are characterized by the application of elements of national power by each disputant upon the other.

Non-violent conflict steps short of violence because absence of the factors that otherwise would make war expedient: either the objective act worth fighting about, or one or both parties lack the requisite power shortage to make a war sufficiently attractive.

Because of the unique role of violence in bringing about absolute solutions to international quarrels, non-violent conflict tends to be inconclusive and productive of only partial victory a partial defeat.

Subversion

Another method of international conflict merits attention in its own right. Since the end of World War II a new dimension has been added to international politics with the elevation of organized subversion to the place of an accepted method of foreign policy. Before 1914 statesmen could confidently expect that although they might be hard put to cope with the pressures exerted by foreign states, three would at least be of a familiar nature and be applied through recognized channels. For the past thirty years, however, it has become a normal procedure for a state to seek to enlist individuals and groups in other countries as its supporters and to set them to work clandestinely to undermine their government and, if possible, to overthrow it.

In self-defence the Western world, led by the United States has set about taking similar counter-measures to subver the Iron Curtain governments and to weaken their grip on their peoples. Thus far the communists have proved more adept in their use of this new weapon.

Effect of Subversion on World Politics. Subversion as a method of international conflict has had at least three perceptible effects upon world politics.

In the first place, it is only by the extensive use of a seductive ideology that a state can win converts of supporters in another country upon a scale broad enough to be worth while. As a result, it has been necessary to tailor ideologies for export in order that they prove sufficiently attractive to peoples of vastly different cultures of attitudes. Current ideological lines of major states therefore place more stress upon fundamental human values and less upon the emotional manifestations of any particular nationalism; failure to make this alteration by a government often renders nugatory the ideological message.

The communist propaganda that serves as a great ferment

throughout much of south and southeast Asia is a far cry from the sophisticated economic principles of Marx and Engels.

Second, the singular importance of wining adherents abroad for purposes of subversion has made it necessary to aim the propaganda activity of major states at particular targets abroad.

Likewise, the USSR makes particular effort to win supporters among the minority groups in the United States who might have reason to be resentful and willing to listen approvingly to Russian propaganda.

In the third place, the severity of the threat from subversion has forced virtually all governments to take strong measures to guarantee their own internal security. Subversive groups have already demonstrated their effectiveness unless protective measures are taken, and every government in the world is alert to the danger.

There has thus been imposed upon free peoples the unfamiliar and unpleasant task of seeking to check subversion by investigating the loyalty of their own citizens.

In the United States this necessity has to some extent played into the hands of a groups of obscurantist and super-patriots who seek by this device to destroy all dissent and to impose a dead conformity.

Conflict of Policies

Conflict arises either from a clash of national policies that reflects a competition of national interest or from a battle of nationalisms the basis of which is not necessarily any divergency of interest. The first is much more common in international politics, but the second, though quantitatively rarer, is potentially more disruptive.

Policy clashes are among the daily occurrences of international affairs. They occur over great questions and small, and involve matters either of vital interest, pheripheral interest, or no real interest at all to one or both states. They cover the whole range of international politics, involving at one time a security question, at another an economic issue, at still another a legal question of jurisdiction or state rights.

Despite the variety of conditions of struggle, it is nevertheless possible to stake out certain general situations from which international policy conflicts arise. They differ from one another primarily in terms of the policies the disputing parties are following at the time they became involved in the controversy. Each type of conflict situation produces a different result because of the variation in the pattern of objectives the different states are seeking.

There are at least three clear types of international conflict situations involving purely policy considerations: first, a conflict arising out of a clash between two states or blocs of states, each of which is following an active expansionist or revisionist policy; second, a conflict between a state seeking to upset the *status quo* and one whose policy is designed for its preservation; third, a conflict involving two *status quo* policies.

Historically a conflict arising between two states both of which are following policies of expansion or revision has proved to be the most dynamic and potentially dangerous to peace of all policy-conflict situations. Usually such parties are driven by powerful motivations and internal stresses in underrating a policy that they know will produce strong opposing reactions. Then a revisionist policy encounters resistance, there is a tendency for the government to increase the pressure.

When two such states conflict, the quarrel is usually marked by the rapid increase in the power each commits to the objective it is seeking and a swift development of tension and crisis. Revisions states also find it extremely difficult to reverse or even to halt policies short to their ultimate objective because of the great internal and international pressures developed.

It is often quite difficult to bring a conflict between two expanding states to a peaceful close. Driven by profound compulsions and often today backed by an aroused nationalism, such states always given serious thought to the expediency of a solution by violence before they will abandon any policy short of its goal.

They usually do not choose war as the means of ultimate resolution, but the choice of some other course that involves policy change is always a difficult one.

Examples of this type of conflict are numerous. One of the most common historical sources has been the struggle between expanding colonial empires. Perhaps the most famous instance of this sort of controversy is the Fashoda incident of 1898.

British imperialism, expanding southward from Egypt to the headwaters of the Nile, clashed with France, expanding eastward across Africa. The overt incident that brought on the crisis occurred at Fashoda on the upper Nile.

Neither side was willing to relinquish its position and for some weeks there was serious talk of war between Great Britain and France. Finally the difference was adjusted, French expansion was directed elsewhere, and the crisis abated.

A more recent example is found in Russo-German relations before World War II. Nazi Germany was wedded to a policy of expansion from the moment the regime was established and Hitler never made any secret of his intention to extend Germany's frontiers and influence into Russian territory.

What he overlooked was the fact that by 1938 the USSR had solved most of its internal problems and was in turn planning to expand westward. The Nazi-Soviet pact of 1939 could not restrain the rival empires; by 1941 fundamental disagreements had multiplied to the point where war was a natural outcome.

A further comment on this type of conflict is suggested by the examples cited. If the expanding policies that conflict at the results of cold and realistic appraisals of the respective national interest, the conflict is unlikely to be of short duration.

Solutions to any particular incident of the struggle are temporary, and the deep-seated problem will continue to flare up again and again until one of the disputing states modifies its policy in some basic way.

The Russo-Japanese quarrel is illustrative. Already over half a century old, no one feels that the conflict is ended; it will be resumed whenever Japan feels that it has recovered adequate strength to make the effort. Both states feel that their national interest is fundamentally involved and each has so far accepted any setback as a mere temporary reversal.

If, on the other hand, an expanding policy that clashes with another is not so clearly identified with a particular interest of a state and does not involve such heavy commitment of emotion and power, the prospects for permanent resolution are a good deal brighter.

Revisionist Vs. Status Quo Policy

The frequently recurring type of conflict situation is that in which an expanding policy collides with the interests of a passive, status quo state. Whereas in the former type of the motives of the disputing parties were basically identical, both seeking to reach the same general objective of an expansion of their authority, in this situation the objectives of the respective states are complimentary.

The revisionist state seeks to take away from the passive state some particular object of advantage, while the latter, seeking nothing, attempts only to retain that which it has already has. The possible objects of such controversy are limitless; practically any aspect of international political life may serve as a pretext.

The expanding state always takes the initiative, seeking by any appropriate means to detach the passive state from its control of the objective; the latter restrains its action to defensive measures, taken each affirmative step of its adversary as it is taken.

For the *status quo* state, an inconclusive end to the conflict is really a victory, since any such outcome leaves it still in possession of the object of the battle. As a result the passive state is ready at any time to terminate the conflict upon the state of the *status quo ante.*

The advantage, assuming the power position of the two

states is approximately equal, lies of necessity with the defensive state, since a drawn battle a victory for it; it need only devise tactics that neutralize the policy of its opponent without necessarily gaining any counter superiority of its own.

It must be always on the power actively pressing its policy, or else its whole cause may be lost. Any state seriously entering into a conflict with a satiated state must have an extraordinary power preponderance before it may contemplate victory, or else be willing to risk the hazardous course of a *blitzkrieg* in order to shatter its resistance before its power can be mobilized.

Impact of World Conditions on Conflicts. Conflicts between state and revisionist powers are to a great extent influenced by the general socio-political climate. When the international order—or at least that segment of it which is involved in the dispute—is relatively stable and there is general satisfaction with the way affairs are arranged, the satiated state enjoys a comparative advantage.

On the other hand, in times of great social change, ideological unrest, or personal insecurity, when accepted value systems are crumbling, strong and aggressive states are more likely to succeed in altering the existing political patterns. The satiated state is less able to count upon support from its associates—many of whom are likely to be having some difficulty in keeping their own houses in order. The climate of world affairs is an important element in determining whether or not a conflict of this sort leads to war.

Other factors may enter in also, including those that always impinge upon any decision of war or peace: the imprudence of the objective to the states concerned and the probability of victory if war were undertaken. It is almost always the aggressive state in this situation that forces the choice of war or peace. The satiated state, having in the possession the disputed objective, has no reason to fight unless such a course is forced upon it by the policy of the other state.

The actual first blow may be struck by the state that had been on the policy defensive, but unless some additional complicating factor enters tree picture the ultimate responsibility for such a war rests upon the expanding state.

The Cold War

Perhaps the greatest and most striking examples of the conflict situation is that furnished by the cold war of the post World War II era.

At the close of the war the United States was in most ways a perfect example of a 'have' state. Its enemies were crushed, its power was unmatched, its ideology was triumphant; it asked for nothing more than to be let alone to execute its self-imposed mission of repairing the damage and destruction caused by the war and of creating a new day of freedom and peace. Its national interest was satisfied to repletion and it had no quarrel with any other state.

The Soviet Union entered the postwar world bent upon a revisionist course. Although its power position and its role in international affairs had improved tremendously—from world pariah to one of the two global giants in a space of twentyeight years was an amazing advance—it was moved by ideological, historical, political, and military considerations to embark upon a course of upsetting the distribution of power to its own advantage.

This policy naturally brought it into conflict with the United States, whose interest in the *status quo* was global and diametrically opposed to that of the Soviet Union. The cold war was the natural result of such a clash of fundamental interests.

The course of the cold war in every way has matched the general description of such passive-active conflict given above. The only difference is one of degree: instead of the struggle being fought over a single objective, the stake is ultimately, which way of life and point of view is to prevail.

Such instances as furnish examples of American initiative in the cold war—for example, the network of American alliances with the states of Europe—have been always tactical for the purpose of gaining a better defensive position. Those respective roles are imposed upon the two states by the requirements of their world policy and the nature of the conflict. American policy must be defensive; popular demand that the United States 'seize the initiative' was based upon a misapprehension of the problem of American foreign policy. As it was the USSR that began the cold war, so it must be the USSR that ends in the United States is prepared at any time to call a half if it were assured that a real change in Soviet policy were in effect, but so long as the fact remains clear that any slackening in our counter-measures would result only in increased Soviet pressure, the cold war must continue.

With the eclipse of the USSR, the scenario of World Politics has changed entirely.

Other Historical Examples. Other historical examples of the dynamic-static conflict are common. Hitler, the aggressor, clashed with satiated Britain and France during the 1930's; bent upon avoiding war, they ought to appease him but only delayed the eventual conflict.

Japan's expansion in Asia during the same period ran a foul of the interests of the 'have' stages in the area—Britain, the United States, France, and the Netherlands—and since Japan was unwilling to limit its objectives war resulted in that case also.

At earlier times in history we find other instance of the would-be conqueror coming into conflict with passive, satisfied states: examples are Napoleon, Frederick the Great, Louis XIV, Charles XII of Sweden, Henry VI of France.

Conflict Between two Passive Politics

When two status quo states, at least in their relations to each other, disagree on great matters or mall international conflict arises. These struggles are seldom so dramatic and never so difficult to handle as the two preceding categories, but altogether this third group constitutes the great bulk of all disagreements in international affairs. In this type of conflict all the parties in dispute share a certain consensus and as a result the struggle only rarely becomes a matter of major policy concern. It remains confined to limits that permit its being dealt with without injury to the over-all programmes of the disputing states.

As a true policy clash, however, it conforms to the general framework of international conflict and is handled in the same way and according to the same principles.

Conflicts of this type are more likely to be procedural in character, involving questions of how relations are to be conducted, rather than the substance of what the relations should be. Being primarily procedural, they are peculiarly amenable to settlement by the more formalized international techniques which employ the rules of international law: mediation, arbitration, or judicial decision. When such a dispute arises out of a deliberate policy decision by one state, it is the least likely of all conflict situations to lead to war. It usually culminates in a mutual adjustment of policies after only the most nominal power clash. This type of struggle is the most 'normal' since it is the inescapable accompaniment of the execution of policy by any state.

The United States and Great Britain have worked in close partnership in all areas of the world in executing projects of great importance and delicacy. This has not, however, eliminated conflict between them; indeed, Anglo-American disagreement upon specifics has been almost as obvious a feature of the partnership as has agreement upon general principles.

On such questions as the recognition of the communist government of China, the partition of India, the partition of Palestine, the Schuman Plan, international trade policy, and the European Defense Community, disagreement and struggle between Britain and the United States has been marked. Yet—and here is the point—in no single instance has conflict been prolonged to the point of creating a rupture in the close alliance.

Each single dispute has been settled or dropped before it has become critical, since both states agree that harmony and co-operation are more importance than any single point of disagreement.

Conflict of Nationalisms

Nationalism, as an inescapable aspect of political life, has a great influence upon the foreign policies of states, and that statesmen seek to control nationalist sentiment and use it in the service of rationally determined objectives.

Hysterical nationalism as a cause of international conflict is the catalyzing element in far fewer international disagreements than is the making of a rational policy decision by a state, but today it constitutes a graver danger to peace. The crisis areas of world politics in the contemporary world are all characterized by a battle of embittered nationalist attitudes. Statesmen find such situations extremely rigid and difficult to control.

It must be admitted that the dichotomy between policy and nationalist conflict is to some extent a false one, since political leadership is everywhere alert to mobilize fanatic popular opinion in its support; but many conflicts are forced upon statesmen by nationalism and go forward by their own emotional momentum without very much calculated direction.

Characteristics of Nationalist Conflict. Nationalism a mass emotion is heedless of what it considers to be the niceties of international politics, and uniformed about the details of the policy either its own government or the government of its enemy is following. It is impatient; once mass emotions are aroused they demand and outlet.

When popular hatred is focused upon a particular state, great pressures are brought to bear upon the government demanding that direct and forceful measures be taken against the offender. It is by its very nature moral in its outlook and imprecise in what it wants except in terms of moralistic and emotional slogans. When two states each embodying such a vigorous nationalist attitude become involved in a dispute, no one can confidently predict the outcome. The relative probabilities of war or peace, which in a situation under the control of statesmen are calculated soberly and realistically, are largely beyond ascertaining.

All sorts of intangibles enter into the situation. The personality and character of the various leaders; the extent to which they can control and, if necessary, oppose public opinion in their respective states; the degree to which the conflict of nationalism is at the same time serving the real interest of one or both parties: all of these factors are beyond measurement but they contribute to the ultimate resolution of the struggle.

Ideologies are always moral, absolute, and mystical; they carry with them an assumption of the unquestionable truth of the propositions they embody and therefore an arrogation of superiority to all who believe over all who do not.

Nationalist conflict thus usually takes the form of the attempt of one group to group its moral, intellectual, or cultural superiority over another. If the other people accept the challenge and seek to do the same in their turn, a battle is joined that is especially bitter because compromise on moral issues is impossible.

The termination of a nationalist conflict by any other means than war is a difficult and often impossible problem. Nationalist hatreds are notoriously unpredictable and a quarrel of peoples may continue for generations, inventing pretexts when no real object of controversy exists.

On the other hand, such a conflict may slowly and gradually disappear after a diminution of intensity over many years, it may suddenly be abandoned with a shift in popular concern to new problems, or it may quite inexplicably evaporate for no perceptible reason.

The Forms of Nationalist Conflict. In the contemporary world several major types of nationalist conflict can be distinguished. Some are two-sides, with both nations displaying the trends and the unyielding attitudes that mark the more pathological variety of nationalism.

Other conflicts are one-sided in that one state is on the psychological offensive and energetically prosecutes nationalist agitation while the other does not make use of such techniques and attempts to confine its relations with the nationalist state within a more rational policy framework. Some of these nationalist struggles have a long history and some are of more recent origin. Some are fought out upon a broad front while others are concentrated within a single overriding issue.

Whatever their special characteristics, however, they are all prosecuted in a highly emotional atmosphere, are fought in ideological terms, and are oriented to an imprecise pattern of objectives. Let us examine at least some of the more conspicuous types of such conflicts.

Historical Animosities

Much of the foreign policy of many states is governed by nationalist animosities' that have a long history. Their origins surrounded in obscurity, they have become to the people a familiar and expected part of the way of doing international business, and governments count upon their continuation in framing their policies. They may lie dormant for long periods only to flare up at critical moments. Their existence imposes great restraint upon a government seeking for practical reasons to establish a closer relationship with the state that is the object of the popular hatred. Most are reciprocal, although some few are unilateral.

(1) *Franco-German Animosity.* The most conspicuous example of such a historical nationalist disagreement is that of France and Germany. This hostility has its origins in the nine century and virtually each generation since has witnessed events that have furnished reasons for the mutual enmity to be deepened.

Today, irrespective of concrete issues, it is axiomatic for many Frenchmen to hate and fear Germans and for many Germans to hate and despise Frenchmen. With this general public attitude to build upon in both states is has been no difficult fear for governments to discover problems that served to intensify the tension.

In the postwar world, the status of the Saar and the question of German rearmament have been the principal points of dispute, but such is the basic unreasonableness of the attitude of the two people— mainly, in the period since 1945, of parts of the French population—that had these issues not presented themselves others would have been found.

Particularly disheartening to men of good will on both sides of the Rhine is that the overriding realities of European politics in the present day make close and intimate Franco-German co-operation a sheer necessity.

French public opinion today is divided; some groups recognize the necessity of abandoning their cherished Teutonophobia if France and the French way of life are to survive, while others find their traditional hatreds a familiar comfort in an uncertain world and stubbornly refuse to adopt different attitudes in the face of crushing necessity.

Although nationalist opposition has slowed the pace of European unification it has not been able to stop the movement entirely; barring a sudden crisis that might recreate the old hatreds in full force, we may look forward to Franco-German nationalist animosity fighting a series of bitter and losing battles with the forces of history and common sense.

(2) *Other European Antipathies.* Western Europe, the birthplace of modern nationalism, affords many other examples of long-lasting nationalist quarrels whose impact upon the states concerned and upon world affairs generally has been of great importance. Their roots are varied; fear, religious and cultural differences, the course of history, economic rivalries, and differences in status all have played a part in particular situations.

Many of them are receding under the soothing influence of time and the imperatives of contemporary political life. Some, however, retain much of their original strength today.

One of the well-established nationalist animosities in Europe is that between Russia and Germany. Originating is basic political differences and buttressed by centuries of bickering, the relations between the governments are often tense and never completely relaxed.

Periods of co-operation between the governments (which have been infrequent) have come about only as a result of overpowering compulsions, and have proved usually to be short-lived.

Other areas of nationalist tension in Europe which might be mentioned include the relations between Germany and Britain, between Britain and France, and Britain and Italy (although the feeling, at least in Mussolini's day, was much stronger on Italy's side than on Britain's).

(3) *Anglo-American Animosity.* Born of the American Revolution and aggravated by a number of contributory factors including the large number and great influence of Irish immigrants into the United States, it underlies much of the day-to-day relations between the two states.

A sizable segment of the populations of both countries is always ready to seize upon any pretext to provoke a nationalist 'twisting the lion's tail'. Many realistic policy decisions of the two governments have to be modified or deferred in difference to this attitude.

Today, the American state of mind toward Britain is made more critical by United States assumption of the burdens of British policy in many parts of the world, by the repeated subsidies given to Britain by the United States, and by what many Americans feel to be a lack of proper gratitude and humility in Britain in return for American aid and leadership.

On the other hand, Britain also has a sensitive nationalism. It is restive under Britain's subordinate position by the dependence of Britain upon American largers, and by what they feel to be an American inability or refusal to live up to the requirements of world leadership.

These are minority attitudes in both states, it is true; but every individual policy disagreement between the two governments is magnified out of its true proportion by these nationalist predispositions with a consequent real effect upon the course of world politics.

(4) *The Balkans.* No discussion of historical nationalist hatreds would be complete without the mention of the complex of

nationalism in the Balkans. Here is found a mixture of national groups, each fired by a frantic patriotic zeal, and each hating and fearing all the others.

Balkan relations have been violent and bitter for three quarters of a century and the rival claims to local predominance and for disputed bits of territory have served to keep Balkan politics a synonym for intrigue, betrayal, and conflict. In the postwar world the normal confusion of the area has been heightened by its inclusion in the critical zone of the cold war.

Bulgaria, Romania, and Albania are Soviet satellites; Yugoslavia was formerly in adherent of the Soviet Union but fell from grace; Greece and Turkey remained in the western sphere. To historical nationalist hatreds were added the complications derived from ideological differences, made more complex because Titoist Yugoslavia, anti-Russian and forced into a pro-Western orientation, nevertheless remained true to its Marxist-Leninist philosophy.

Colonial Revolutions and their Aftermath

The most prominent type of nationalist conflict that is common today has its origin in a successful colonial revolution. No subject people can become free of alien control without first developing a keen sense of nationalistic particularism and making the achievement of independence the primary order of business.

Once the revolution has been accomplished, the hatreds created by the struggle live on and form a significant part of the foreign policy of the new state.

Sometimes the predisposition toward conflict is directed entirely toward the former imperial master; more often it is a broader attitude, which encompasses all states that are associated with the former ruler or that have similar policies.

The Asiatic revolutions of the postwar period have left the new states with a very strong anti-white and anti-imperialist nationalistic bias. That these attitudes are not unique to the generation that accomplished the revolution but may be transmitted for many years until they become a matter of historical tradition is indicated by the persistence of the anti-British feeling both in the United States and among the Boers of South Africa.

The aftermath of a colonial revolution is often such as to make the re-establishment of close relations and policy co-operation between the former ruler and the new state difficult or impossible.

Newly won independence is a cherished thing; even its insignificant external manifestations are made much of and new states are peculiarly sensitive to real or imagined slights. The pride of the people who have recently gained independence often forces them to demand foreign policies from their government that run counter to basic requirements of the state. Modern colonial revolutions do not end with the termination of political relationships; they often involve wholesale uprooting of long-standing economic and cultural ties as well.

This serves to make affairs somewhat chaotic within the new state; the people, finding the freedom is not the unalloyed boon they had expected it to be, discover in their former sovereign a convenient scapegoat upon whom to vent their frustrations.

What is true for the formal rupture of political imperialism applies also in cases where the independence acquired is economic in nature, or merely the freedom from informal tutelage, some of the states of the Middle East have been technically independent for over a generation, but Arab nationalism is a fairly recent growth since World War II.

Its target has been British and French economic domination of the area and the destruction of the privileged role of Britain as 'adviser' to the Arab governments. Although the situation has many local peculiarities, the general tenor of Arab anti- British feeling is exactly what one would expect in a people recently freed from colonial status.

The Arab governments often follow an anti-British course even when the reverse would clearly be to their real advantage. This has served to complicated United States relations in this region, since the close Anglo-American partnership serves, in

Arab minds, to contaminate the United States with the virus of colonialism also.

Asian Nationalism. In the modern world the major colonial revolutions have taken place in Asia. Although the colonial powers who saw their empires shrink and disappear in the backwash of World War–II. Great Britain, France, the United States, and the Netherlands— varied in the alacrity with which they recognized the new situation and in the degree of resistance they offered to the trend toward independence, none of them displayed very much nationalist animosity toward their departing subject.

The hatred was all on the other side, and has continued almost unabated to the present. By and large the populations of the new Asiatic states are suspicious and hostile toward their former masters— least of all are the Filipino people toward the United States—and in addition their colonical experiencc has coloured their over-all.

Racial, Religious, Social, and Cultural Issues

Another group of nationalist conflicts that plague contemporary world politics arises out of a complex of causes that we may generalize as racial, religious, social, and or cultural. In this type, the issues are often trivial in themselves, and if rational analysis were applied to them satisfactory solutions usually could quite easily be worked out.

The specific objects of controversy are often merely symbols of ideological differences. Settlement upon the basis of compromise would, in the minds of the people, involve concessions upon points of fundamental moral significance. This they generally refuse to consider. No conflict situation is more difficult to deal with, either by the statesmen concerned who wish to keep it within bounds and directed toward valid policy objectives or by the outside states seeking to end the struggle in the interests of peace.

Such a conflict tends to run its own course, whether short or long, and seldom ends suddenly. The termination of such struggles comes about usually because one or both of the nationalisms involved finds other issues to become concerned about and the one that caused the trouble is simply abandoned.

Racial and Religious Conflict. An apt example of a racial root to a nationalist controversy is the dispute between India and the Union of South Africa, involving the treatment of the Indian population of the Union.

South Africa's racial policies were a matter of world concern, but only India had the opportunity to join the battle directly. The conflict, although officially waged in a restrained manner through the formal channels of diplomacy and in the United Nations, has been a matter of profound nationalist conviction on both sides.

India sees in this dispute the culmination of years or resentment toward the claims to superiority made by the white race; the Union of South Africa claims its policy is the only way possible to preserve the peculiar values of white civilization against the encroachments of other races.

The involvement of religion in nationalist disputes is all too common both in history and in present-day international politics.

Western hostility toward the Ottoman Empire in the nineteenth century was to a large extent the result of Christian hatred of Mohammedans; Irish Anglophobia is the partial product of religious differences; Argentine spurning of 'Yanqui' policy is buttressed by a distrust of a predominant American Protestantism; the Middle East crisis of the past few years has been intensified by Arab-Jewish religious disagreement.

It is seldom that a religious issue is the principle admitted cause of a nationalist conflict (although for millions of Americans the most damning charge that can be made against the Soviet Union is its promotion of atheism and its semi-official attitude that 'religion is the opiate of the masses'), but it is often a contributory element and has a strongly moving effect upon the emotions of a people.

Social and Cultural Conflicts. Social and cultural questions also contribute their share to nationalist disagreements. Involving as it does the whole matter of a 'way of life,' this last category is the most vague and lacking in specific terms of all the classes of conflict.

Europeans generally have had an unfavourable reaction to United States leadership in the cold war. Barred by their pride from a candid recognition that European weakness itself is the reason for American entry into European affairs, they have discovered an outlet for many of their resentments in a nationalist campaign against the intrusion of American cultural standards into their society.

The United States is castigated as the home of a 'Coca-Cola' civilization, as materialistic and insensitive, as worshipping wealth, size, and strength to the exclusion of intelligence, creative and critical ability, and sophistication.

American civilization is claimed to be mass-produced, mediocre, and destructive of all the civilized amenities.

Americans, on their part, often consider Europeans soft, decadent, corrupt, and incapable to ordering their own affairs. There is a tendency in the United States to feel that the historical roles at last are reversed and that the time has come for Europe to discard its pretensions and to learn the lesson of freedom and democracy from its new master, the United States.

Of course, neither set of arguments deserves to be taken seriously on its own merits, but one must realize that this cultural conflict has seriously coloured United States relations with the states of western Europe. The pernicious effect of these nationalist attitudes has reached government circles on both sides of the Atlantic with unfortunate policy results.

Incomplete reports indicate that something of the same controversy is going on inside the Soviet empire. Russian pan-Slavism has always argued that the Russians are the 'great Slavs' and thus the natural preceptors and protectors of the 'lesser Slay' peoples.

Implicit in this attitude is the assumption of the superiority of Russian cultural values over those of the smaller states. Since 1917 this historic point of view of the Russian people has been strengthened by the 'monopoly of truth' which Marxist-Leninist -Stalinist ideology purports to possess. Since the war, Russian cultural pretensions have been impressed upon the European satellites in no subtle fashion; it has long been clear to the minor partners of the USSR that they are expected to make themselves over into exact copies of the Russian state and society.

This has met with great, although sub rosa, opposition by the peoples of eastern Europe. They have proved to be remarkably stubborn in clinging to their own ways of life.

Expanding Nationalisms in Conflict

A final situation out of which nationalist conflict grows is that which makes so much of today's world politics tense and threatening; the clash of expanding great-power nationalisms. When a people with a "universalist" outlook on the world happen to occupy a state having great power resources, a powerful dynamic element is injected into world politics.

When two such states are simultaneously in existence, each supporting its nationalist aspirations with power, even an inexperienced observer could accurately forecast serious and long-lasting conflict.

This situations has recurred not infrequently. French and British nationalism clashed in the Napoleonic era (and many times previously); Austrian and Russian nationalisms in the matter part of the nineteenth century. Today, the rival nationalism, each with its own imperialistic overtones, are the Russian and the American.

What is more important for our purposes in the effect that this clash of nationalisms has upon the over all course of international politics.

Policy Consequences of Nationalist Conflict. The cold war is more than a pure nationalist disagreement. Earlier in this chapter we painted out that the Soviet-American conflict was an inevitable outcome of the particular policies adopted by the two states after the defeat of the Axis. Nationalist attitudes intensify the struggle the struggle, however, and tend to perpetuate it; the concrete policy disagreements are often lost sight of and largely forgotten in the preoccupation of both groups with the nationalist battle. Policy conflicts are difficult or impossible to resolve as long as each side identifies itself with virtue incarnate and its opponent as the personification of evil.

So long as this nationalist orientation is maintained on both sides the lessening of the tensions of the cold war is scarcely to be expected. The existence of the rival nationalisms has served to block the attempts of each ideology to achieve universal acceptance.

Prevented by Russian propaganda from convincing the Russian people of the inherent superiority of the United States, American nationalism had shifted its sights and concentrates instead upon proving the same point to the other states of the free world.

The results of the forcible Americanization of Europe and free Asia were alluded to earlier: an immediate resentment and resistance on the part of the people of the other areas, followed by a demand for policy re-orientation by their governments in order to escape from American domination.

Soviet nationalism has had the same experience. Unable to find fertile ground to spread the message outside the Iron Curtain, it has perforce been obliged to preach Russian supremacy to its own allies.

No sober or neutral analyst could reach any other conclusion than that imperialist, expanding nationalism is a self-defeating policy. Not only has neither the Soviet Union nor the United States convinced the other of the correctness of its ideology, the strength of its institutions, or the inevitability of its eventual triumph; instead both discover today that outside their own borders there are fewer people who believe in the claims of either or both of them than there were before they set about trying to convince them.

An expanding nationalism serves usually to inflame the nationalist attitudes of other states and to stir up animosities that had not previously been active.

A growing impatience with the recklessness and dynamism of both great powers is already apparent in many parts of the world. Whether this will culminate in a concentrated effort to quell the great-power rivalry before it brings the world to war or merely in a futile attempt of other peoples to declare their neutrality as between the two giants, no one can yet tell.

One thing, however, is clear; the clash of the expanding nationalisms of the United States and the Soviet Union is the most unsettling and dangerous feature of world politics today.

It has become clear throughout the foregoing discussion that the categories of nationalist conflict are not exclusive, nor is the distinction between policy conflict and nationalist conflict always evident.

The various types of nationalist controversy shade into one another; racial and religious issues are involved, for instance in the quarrel between the Netherlands and Indonesia.

Nationalist, as a mass emotion, does not lend is self easily to objective analysis, and many of the distinctions drawn in the discussions in this chapter are those of emphasis and degree rather than of kind. But despite the imprecise description of an imprecise phenomenon, the whole subject of nationalist conflict points one great moral.

International conflict is susceptible to control when it arises out of the reasoned judgments of statesmen. It escapes from control and may lead anywhere at all when it arises from the interplay of nationalist emotions which call into question the most basic attitudes and beliefs of entire peoples.

The Organization of Power in the World Today

For the purposes of more effective prosecution of policy, the leading states of the world today have sought with some success to organize large multi-state power blocs.

This is not a novel development in international politics; as we have seen a very few states feel themselves sufficiently strong to seek to accomplish their ends without assistance.

Alliances and power groupings of all sorts have been a feature of world affairs even since the beginning of the national-state system.

The present basis of organization of power in the world differs materially from that of earlier periods, however, on two grounds. In the first place, contemporary alliances are geographically much more extensive and organizationally more elaborate than at any earlier time. The great antagonists of the contemporary era have attempted to bring all the states of the world into one camp or the other and to bind them there with detailed institutional arrangements. Second, each of the power blocs of the world is organized around a single leader.

The relations between the principal member of each group and all its other members are supposed to be those of director and subordinates. This latter condition has not been altogether happy; a constant feature of each major alliance is the internal struggle as each of the lesser members seeks to gain some great measure of independence at action.

World Power Structure. The world today is divided into two great power blocs. Despite the inherent instability of international relationships, which makes each group somewhat less firmly organized than might appear from the formal treaty arrangements, they nevertheless given most of the states of the world a general policy orientation which underlies most of their policy. These groupings are of course the alliance of the 'free world' and the communist bloc.

Between them they include the great majority of the people of the world and a clear preponderance of its political power. Not included in either alliance, and seeking to establish a basis for action, are the so-called 'neutrals.' This third group hopes to preserve its independence and to remain upon passable terms with both great alliances.

The 'Free World' Alliance

The United States. The alliance of the free (non-communist) world, the United States has played the critical role. The creation of the network of alliance grew in the first instance out of American policy, and the economic, military, and political strength of the United States has provided the organizing and directing force. We have hoped to organize all the non-communist, democratic states of the world into a grouping that could successfully resist any further expansion of communist power. By construction such a bulwark against Soviet expansionism, United States policy has aimed at securing the support and assistance of its allies in the prosecution of purely American policies. The 'Free world' is not a monolithic entity; it does not consist of a single massive whole which thinks and acts as a unit. Even if such an arrangement had been possible, it would have been undesirable.

Membership in each alignment includes the United States and those states with common interests in the region or the problem. When possible, these alliances are multilateral; in several instances, however, it has proved necessary to conclude arrangements with individual states.

The United States has encouraged its allies to negotiate supplementary treaties with each other and occasionally with other states not directly included within the American orbit.

The alliances led by the United States are basically similar. They are almost all 'mutual defence' pacts which provide for assistance and cooperative action in case of crisis.

They also generally provide for mutual assistance in building defences against communist pressure; this in practice means that the United States undertakes to make available to its allies various forms of aid—economic, military, and technical. Another common feature is the commitment entered into by the membership that all disputes arising among them will be settled by pacific means.

This serves a double purpose; it ensures peaceful relations

among the United States and its allies, and it reduces the possibility that the communist bloc might disrupt the alliance by exploiting differences of opinion within it.

The North Atlantic Treaty (NATO). Perhaps the keystone of the structure of the free world, and certainly the most elaborately organized alliance within it, is the North Atlantic Treaty. This agreement became effective in August 1949, between the United States, Canada, and ten western European states: Belgium, Denmark, France, Iceland, Italy, Luxembourg, the Netherlands, Norway, Portugal, and the Great Britain. In February 1952, Greece and Turkey announced their adherence; in May 1955, West Germany entered also.

It was hoped that this alliance would bring together the principal allies of the United States and a number of key European states into a solid and manageable groupings. It has served as the basis upon which much of our later policy, both in Europe and elsewhere, has been built.

The treaty is founded upon the principle that an armed attack against one or more of the signatories 'in Europe or North America shall be considered an attack against them all.' Here is a clear obligation to cooperate in the event of war. Other provision stipulate rearmament through self-help and mutual aid, and regular and frequent consultation upon common problems. To execute the treaty, there was created in April 1952 the North Atlantic Treaty Organization (NATO). This is the formal operating agency which carries out the provisions of the treaty.

NATO is organized at three levels. At the top is the North Atlantic Council, made up of civilian political representatives at the ministerial level. This body, responsible for over-all policy, is aided by a permanent international staff headed by a Secretary-General.

The next level of NATO includes the Military Committee (national representatives) and the Standing Group (military personnel on permanent assignment). These groups are responsible for detailed plans of operation to execute the treaty. The 'operational' level of NATO consists of its field military commands, including one for Europe (SACEUR) and one for the North Atlantic area (SACLANT).

The North Atlantic Treaty itself declares that the alliance was created pursuant to Article 51 of the Chapter, which recognizes that every member has the inherent right to engage in ' individual or collective self-defence! It is perfectly clear that one of the inspirations for NATO was a conviction that the United Nations is insufficiently strong to provide a security guarantee against the USSR, and the treaty seeks to fill this deficiency. As might be expected, the Soviet Union claims that NATO is contrary to the Charter, being an instrument of aggression against Russia; more serious is the accusation made by many serious scholars that NATO is not in the spirit of the United Nations.

Regional alliances are supposed to supplement United Nations action, not to replace it. In any case, however, there has not been any widely based move to challenge the compatibility of NATO and the Charter, although the questions continue to be debated.

The Organization of American States. The Western Hemisphere is also organized originally into a great alliance. Known as the Organization of American States, the alliance is based upon the Inter-American Treaty of Mutual Assistance, signed at Rio de Janeiro in 1947. The Organization itself went into effect in 1951. The Rio Treaty served as the general model for the later North Atlantic Pact and it contains the same kinds of guarantees. Collective-security understanding, involving mutual consultation and aid in the event of security threats to a member, form its central idea. There are also included pledges of pacific settlement of disputes arising among the membership and provisions for self-help and mutual aid in building up effective hemisphere defence. The organizational apparatus of the Organization of American States is not so elaborate as for NATO. In the first place, no unified military commands exist within the Western Hemisphere and therefore nothing similar to HAPE or SACLANT can be found.

The emphasis of the OAS is upon regular consultation and policy co-ordination, rather than upon unified military action by the membership, and consequently the central agency of the Organization is the periodic (every five years) conference of all member states.

A central headquarters with a permanent staff is maintained, and various agencies for communication and co-operation in limited fields are now operating.

ANZUS. A third regional organization was put into effect by the United States in 1952, when a mutual-defence treaty between the United States, Australia, and New Zealand became operative. ANZUS, as the new grouping came to be known, was created as a result of the need to organize the Pacific region to meet the evolving communist threat there. Discussion centered for a time upon the possibility of forming a general Pacific pact, to include as many anti-communist states as could be induced to join, but eventually this idea was rejected in favour of the creation of ANZUS plus a series of bilateral pacts involving particular Asian nations.

ANZUS brings together three states whose governments, cultures, and objectives are basically similar, and frees the alliances from the complications that would arise if Asian states, with their complex heritage of colonialism, were include. ANZUS is organized more or less like a simpler NATO. An ANZUS Council, composed of the foreign ministers of the three states, sets general policy; military and political co-operation grows out of these arrangements. Consultation among military staff representatives and programmes of mutual aid in the defence of the Pacific area constituted its major business during its first year of existence.

Bilateral Treaties

The United States has also negotiated several bilateral security agreements with states that, for one reason or another, could not be included within a regional grouping. By means of such arrangements, these individuals stages have been brought into the general framework of the free world and contribute their particular increments of strength to the common effort.

These bilateral treaties are similar in effect to the multilateral ones previously discussed, providing for mutual assistance in resisting attack, for friendship and co-operation, and for mutual military and economic assistance. A considerable amount of American aid has been made available to individual states under the terms of these agreements.

Among such bilateral arrangements is included the Security Pact with Japan, dating from September 1951. The relationship was clouded by the terms of the Japanese Constitution of 1947, which forbade that nation ever to maintain armed forces except for internal police purposes.

Accordingly the major provision of the Japanese-American agreement simply conferred upon the United States the right to maintain armed forces within Japan. Later, as it became obvious that the permanent disarmament of Japan was unworkable and undesirable in view of the development of the cold war, the United States initiated programmes looking forward to eventual rearmament of its erstwhile enemy.

The first such agreement, providing for American aid to Japanese military forces, was reached in August 1953.

Other mutual-defence treaties made by the United States include those with the Republic of the Philippines (March 1952), with Republic of Korea (August 1953), and with Spain (September 1953). Each of these has its special problems.

The Korean treaty, for example, was hammered out during the period of crisis preceding the negotiation of the final armistice ending the Korean war, and tied the United States to a truculent and potentially troublesome ally.

The agreement with Spain, on the other hand, is of only limited scope; it grants the United States land for the development of air bases in return for American economic and military assistance to Spain.

SEATO. The most recent regional grouping to become formalized is the Southeast Asia Treaty Organization, which became a reality on 7 September 1954, when eight states signed a mutual-defence agreement covering that region of the world. The signatories included the United States, the Philippines, France, Pakistan, Thailand, Britain, Australia, and New Zealand. The treaty, immediately known in the United States as SEATO, is designed to protect southeast Asia from any attempted aggression. Although termed a Southeast Asia defence treaty, the list of adherents reveals that only three Asian states participated in framing the document; the rest of the allies are states of Western culture.

The greater part of non-communist Asia forms part of the 'neutral' bloc, whose leaders are India, Indonesia, and Myanmar.

These states, as fearful of renewed Western imperialism as they are of the threat of communism, refused to join SEATO until they became convinced that its purposes are genuinely peaceful and in their own interest.

Even so, SEATO is not as strong a document as many had originally hoped for. It provides for join action against 'aggression', but not specifically against communist aggression. This is a gesture toward those states that feared an open provocation to China.

Another point of relative weakness would seen to be provision that each state shall meet a crisis 'according to its constitutional processes'; this would mean that no automatic obligation is assumed by any signatory.

Such an arrangement is much less stringent than that a NATO. A third shortcoming is the absence of provisions creating any enforcement mechanisms; action to create such agencies was begun in 1955. Despite these objections, however, the mere creation of SEATO served to close a large gap in the ring of alliances the United States has attempted to extend around the communist empire. The treaty became a matter of high priority following the Indo-China debacle in the summer of 1954, and to get the alliance created so soon after such a communist victory was a diplomatic stroke of much significance.

If it proves workable and sufficiently attractive in its economic implications to tempt the Asian neutrals toward the camp of the West, SEATO may yet turn out to be a major stone in the structure of the free world.

Middle East Defence Command. Though it is yet only a project for negotiation rather than detailed plan, the United States is attempting to create a Middle East Defence Command.

This proposed alliance would lie the United States and Britain with the small states of the region in a single organization for mutual defence. Although prosecuted by the United States for several years, the proposal has not had much encouragement.

Several complications have impeded its realization. Perhaps the most significant has been the continuation of tension between Israel and the Arab states, growing out of the former's successful war of independence. Other obstacles have arisen out of Arab resentment at Britain, stemming from the Israel war, the Anglo-Iranian oil dispute, and the Suez Canal question.

Resolution of the last two of these quarrels during 1954 seemed to brighten ultimate prospects for an over-all agreement at some later time. Underlying much of the Arab resistance to the idea is a vigorous nationalism which prefers recently won—although perilous—independence of action to membership in an organization that would inevitably be under Western leadership.

Here again the ghost of a dead imperialism has impaired effective co-operation. Despite these difficulties however, the United States is continuing its effort to organize the Middle East.

The Russo-Chinese Alliance

One of the major mysteries of recent world politics is the exact nature of the relations between the Russia and the government of communist China. The victory of the Chinese communists in 1949 was the most impressive increase in communist strength since the 1917 Bolshevik revolution in Russia.

The Soviet Union moved swiftly to capitalize upon this advantage. In February 1950 a treaty of friendship and mutual assistance was signed in Moscow between the two communist Titans.

Economic agreements which provide for the exchange of commodities and military protocols regarding the training and equipping of Chinese troops have been negotiated. In addition, there is evidence that other, secret understandings have been reached involving co-ordination of policies in particular situations. Despite the outward appearances of harmony, buttressed by incessant parade of ideological unity, the Western world has come to wonder about the solidarity of the Russo-Chinese relationship. Fundamental points of rivalry and disagreement have never been up, and considerable suspicion remains that China is unwilling to remain indefinitely in the subordinate role of Moscow intends for its to play.

The death of Marshal Stalin in March 1953 removed the Russian whom the Chinese recognized as an ideological and political superior, and since then China has asserted its independence more aggressively. The Korean truce of 1953 and the Indo-China truce of 1954 were both more in harmony with Chinese wishes them with those of the Soviet.

What the future holds for the Russo-Chinese alliance we can only guess. Disruptive forces are present, but we dare not underestimate the cohesive force of ideologies and of common enemies and dangers.

Whether Moscow can sustain a close working relationship with an ally that insists upon being considered an equal remains to be seen. If a viable basis for co-operation cannot be worked out, it is clear that the power structure of the world will undergo a major change. In a unipolar world after dismemberment of the USSR this alliance may challenge the supremacy of the US which is the real demand of the hour. By inclusion of India in this nexas the scenario of world politics may go a new turn.

5

Concept of International Community

The constituent part of the state, the individual human being, is a 'political animal' pure and simple. Man as citizen is considered to have no interests of motivations other than those that arise from his membership in a political group, and he is supposed to discover complete personal fulfilment in the performance of his civic duties.

The fact of human nature, however, run contrary to this operating hypothesis of statesmen. Despite the great increase in the functions of government there remains a vast area of individual activity that is 'non-political': that is, it is either untouched by the state or else governmental intervention is unhappy or a total failure.

Men simply cannot, despite the efforts of the most totalitarian of dictators, live all their lives within the arms of the state. Growing out of this failure of political authority to achieve true totality and as a result of the greater impetus.

Provided by the expanding technology of our time, more and more individuals have had their lives touched by other individuals from different states.

Although by no means of equal effect in every case, this increase in private international relationships has served in some measure to diminish the more extreme effects of nationalist bias in many people.

This effect has not been ignored by governments. Those that have had the greatest interest in the perpetuation of intense nationalist rivalry have been most active in attempting to reduce the frequency of private international contacts.

The government of the USSR, whose principal domestic propaganda line had been to insist that the Russian peoples have nothing in common with those of the capitalist world, has been the worst offender in this regard, closely followed by the government of Communist China.

Nevertheless, despite the cold war and other restrictive policies of governments, private international relationships have been expanding and have grown to the point where they perceptibly affect the political relations of states.

As people representing different states and cultures come into contact in pursuit of common objectives, they frequently discover that the cultural then Furnaces between them become less glaring and their common humanity group in importance.

The resulting cooperative attack upon individual non-plodical problems has been responsible for the creating of many organizations, composed of citizens of different states and oriented toward the mutual states faction of private ends.

When an individual is involved in such an activity, he cannot escape undergoing a basic readjustment in his political outlook. He can no longer think of foreign states as corporate entities or political abstractions; Great Britain, France, of Japan ceases to be monolithic structure but instead is thought of as a collection of individual human beings very much like himself.

Individual International Relationships

It is one of the many paradoxes of modern political life that the present day, in which the role of the state and the compelling force of nationalism have grown to the highest level in history, has at the same time witnessed the greatest multiplication of private international relationships. As citizens, men are urged on every side to forsake all international identification (except perhaps with those other states with which good relations are temporarily important to their government) and to adhere only to their state and to their own national group.

In their private lives, however, more and more of them have experienced some form of personal contact with other peoples. This, to many, serves to make the conflict between private interest and public (national) interest more real and more poignant.

The trend at the present time is unquestionably in the direction of a continued intensification in the conflict, because governments today are not yet ready to relax much of their grip upon the loyalties of men.

Transportation and Communication

The main reason for the increase in international contact is the fact that the world has grown smaller. Modern devices of transportation and communication have made any part of the world immediately accessible by radio, telephone, or wireless communication, while no portion of the globe is more than a few hours away from any other point by rapid air transportation. A good deal of what has been written and said about man's conquest of space and time either has been hackneyed and platitudinous or else has ignored its broader implications for civilization. Nevertheless, the facts are clear for all to see: many people have taken immediate advantage of these rapid and relatively inexpensive methods of broadening their personal horizons. All areas of human social life are affected by these devices.

Economic life has been greatly transformed and the social, religious, and recreational activities of individuals in most of the world have been revolutionized by the radio and the airplane.

Transportation. Rapid transportation is so much a commonplace or contemporary life in Western society that most of us realize only vaguely how it has changed the very tempo of our civilization. Today the airplane has revolutionized concepts of distance. In 1952 the British Overseas Aircraft Company placed in service the first scheduled jet passenger airliner; its elapsed.

To cross the Atlantic in the eighteenth century required weeks of uncomfortable and dangerous sailing; today modern steamship make the crossing in less than four days and aircraft in only twelve hours.

Thus, London is closer to New York today than Philadelphia was at the time of the Revolution.

Of only slightly less importance in the development of easy rapid transportation have been the railway and the automobile. There are over 7,80,000 miles of railway track age in the world, the bulk in the United States and Western Europe; particularly in the latter area has the railway served to expedite the expansion of private international contacts.

Since the construction of hard-surfaced highways, the privately owned automobile has also worked major changes in the range of mobility of individuals. In 1949, there were over 62 million automobiles registered in the world, of which 44 million were in the United States.

The means that, granted the curiosity of the human species, more and more individuals will take advantage of the opportunity to travel—for whatever reason—as facilities are improved. Statistics confirm this hypothesis.

The constant increase in the employment of air facilities for the international travel means that more people are crossing frontiers by air at the time and in the consummation of their business are making the personnel contact and are receiving the impressions that are inevitable. Similar increase are notable in steamship traffic and upon international railways.

Communication. Anyone within reach of a telephone can speak with any other part of the world within a few moments, and technical improvements are being made steadily. There are roughly 65 million telephone instruments in the world, scattered over all continents and in most countries, all tied to gather into one vast network. International telegraphs and cable facilities provide another means of rapid communication.

By these devices personal communication between

individuals becomes extremely easy and rapid; international postal service by air has served again to reduce drastically the time required to exchange more detailed communication by letter mail. Of equal, although different, significance is the great expansion of the devices of mass, as opposed to individual communication. The most important of these are the radio and the motion pictures. Radio waves know no frontier, and particularly in Europe, where the political units are so small, any regular radio listener is offered a broad international menu of programmes to suit his taste. Even in the United States, home radio receivers have become so powerful that to receive broadcasts from Europe, South America, or even Asia is a common place for millions of Americans. Motion pictures also exert a great influence upon the international attitudes of people everywhere. The American motion-picture industry has played the leading role in the internationalization of the film. American-made productions go all over the world, into Europe and Asia and Africa, carrying with them their message of the American way of life; revenue from foreign bookings bulks large in the calculations of American producers.

Lately, the process has been somewhat reversed; films are being made in foreign locations by American companies (largely because of restrictions upon currency exchange) and thus American audiences are furnished visual demonstration of the physical and human backgrounds of foreign countries, all without ever leaving home.

The international movement of motion pictures has been made more nearly mutual since World War II as British, French, Italian, German, and some Japanese films have obtained mass audiences in the United States.

Improved transportation and communications are themselves necessarily conducive to greater international understanding. It is clearly easier today for many people to establish contact with individuals in other states and more and more people are doing so. Whether this is for good or ill depends of course upon the circumstances of the particular relationship.

Economic Interdependence

The frontiers of states are drawn in response to a number of forces, both historical and contemporary; only rarely do they enclose a territory sufficiently well balanced economically to maintain a high standard of living within the state.

Despite the efforts of certain governments in recent years to achieve economic self-sufficiency, the various parts of the world stand in a relation of economic interdependence if the resources of modern industrial production are to be exploited to their maximum advantage for all individuals everywhere. In the face of much political control of international economic life, trade reflecting these mutual needs continues to move; in the process, individuals follow their commerce. No relationship is more universally human than that of buying and selling; in the conduct of international trade some of the closest and most lasting international private relationships are created.

Coffee and sugar and petroleum from Latin America; rubber and tin from Southeast Asia; wool from Australia; newsprint from Canada: all of these commodities impinge directly upon the lives of individual Americans and made them, however accidentally, participants in the international community.

Exports tell the same story. Although exports represented in 1950 only approximately 7 per cent of total United States production—the lowest percentage since 1935—the 10 billion dollars' worth of trade they formed was not a inconsiderable factor in retaining the high level of United States prosperity.

Where American products go in quantity, there must go also American technicians, salesmen, and other necessary personnel. Thus the process of importing and exporting commodities, made necessary buy the economic interdependence of the states of the world, brings people into international contact in two ways.

In the first place, products that come from beyond American frontiers or that go outside them play a large part in the lives of those who either produce or consume them; the lives of every one of us would be vastly poorer if we were forced to dispense with all such commodities.

In the second place, the exchange of goods across frontiers involves many people in the process, and these individuals participate in the creation of a real working international understanding at a highly personal level.

Other States. A similar statistical story could be related of most of the other states of the world. Some of the main participants in world politics must import many more vital commodities than does the United States. Great Britain, for example, imports approximately half of its basic foodstuffs, including meat and cereals; France must normally import the great bulk of coal; Italy must import both coal and iron ore, in addition to a large amount of food.

Politicians may seek, for good reasons or ill, to create self-sufficient enclaves within the borders of their states, but at best this is extremely difficult and possible only at the cost of serious dislocations in the lives of private citizens.

It is a fact of contemporary politics in many parts of the world—especially western Europe—that individuals are growing increasingly doubtful of the wisdom of choosing nationalist autarky over the improved standard of living possible through international economic cooperation.

Opening of Underdeveloped Areas

The Underdeveloped Areas. Closely allied to the general situation of the economic interdependence of peoples as a factor in the augmentation of international private contacts is the special case of the recent opening of the underdeveloped areas of the world to modern techniques.

In Asia, Africa, the Middle East, and Latin America, the period since 1945 has witnessed the initiation of extensive two-way contact and communication between these great portions of the world and Western civilization.

In the first place, most of them were resented from the

mainstream of either private or public international life; they were largely unaware of what went on outside their boundaries, and the remainder of the world to a great extent reciprocated this ignorance. Secondly, either they were all colonies of imperialist state or, although technically independent, they had never economically or politically emerged from a colonial orientation; that is, nationalist self-consciousness was only imperfectly developed and self-government was either nonexistent or very ineffective. Third, they uniformly possessed low standard of living and made only extremely inefficient use of their natural and human resource endowment Social and economic discontent, although usually submerged, was widespread because of flagrant inequities in the distributions of the rewards of the society.

Since the end of the war these areas have all erupted. Politically and economically they have suddenly broken out into the main stream of world affairs and have attempted each in its own way, to initiate an attack upon the world political community had suddenly increased its membership by some two dozen states.

The 'underdeveloped' peoples refuse to be taken for granted any more and their impact upon international life is already great and will continue to grow. For Americans particularly, the appearance of these areas upon the world scene has been a revelation. It has become a matter of sheer necessity for us to make contact with peoples of completely different cultures and to learn the requirements for continuing to live in the same world with them.

Problems of political, economic, and racial adjustment have pressed upon us simultaneously with the obligation to gain some sort of factual education about what sort of people these are.

Most of our historical contacts with foreigners have been with Europeans, whose value systems and cultural backgrounds spring from the same roots as do our own. Copping with states such as India and Indonesia, Iran and Egypt, all of whom have revolted against Western imperialism, has forced us to re-evaluate many of our own assumptions in order to discover that approach which will procure a sympathetic hearing for our own case.

Political Contacts. In the political field, the fact that almost all these states are now executing their own foreign policies with near-belligerent independence has in itself increased their impact upon the rest of the world. India, Pakistan, Burma, the Philippines, and many other similar states now for the first time maintain diplomatic relations with most of the other governments in the world.

Natives of these states thus come into direct contact with the governmental machinery and the cultural flow of all Western states, with an in companying acceleration in the education of all concerned.

This effect is tightened by the fact that the diplomats of the new states are all drawn from the leadership class in their homelands and exert an influence out of proportion to their small numbers.

The process of acculturation also works in reverse. Foreign states maintain diplomatic establishments in each of the new states and the citizens of the younger governments come into contact with official representatives of many cultures of which they had previously been only vaguely aware. It must be repeated that this process of accommodation in the political field is a mutual one.

The industrialized West must accept the fact of an independent East that is determined to be treated as an equal, but so must the new states rid themselves of some of their most deep-seated and erroneous antipathies toward Western civilization.

The attainment of full political understanding and cooperation can be possible only upon a basis of fundamental inter cultural adjustment.

Economic Contacts. In the area of economic life the underdeveloped areas and the Western world have come into the closest and most intimate contact. Before 1941, the economic resources of these territories were, generally speaking, under the direct exploitation of western capitalists; since then, the inhabitants have to a considerable degree taken over the determination of their own economic destinies.

This has been an enlightening experience for everyone concerned. The problems of production, transportation, and distribution of the commodities produced and their exchange for other products in the markets of the world have proved both more complicated and more simple than originally imagined.

Technical knowledge of production is often lacking among these peoples, as is also experience in marketing and distributing the goods produced.

The outside world has had in turn to learn the peculiar way of doing business followed by the relatively inexperienced representatives of these areas. The Western world and the underdeveloped areas are coming into wider economic contact than ever before and each has a great deal to learn from the others. It has not been a process altogether easy and happy, but it has been a necessary one that promises to continue for a long time.

The programme of technical assistance and co-operation with the underdeveloped areas undertaken by the United States—known as 'Point IV' from its inclusion as the last point in a four-part American foreign policy by President Truman in 1949—is perhaps the most ambitious and well-tensioned policy followed by any Western government in dealing with the new states. It is based upon the unquestioned need of these areas for the kind of technical economic assistance that only the West can provide.

It proceeds upon a completely voluntary on the part of the state requesting the assistance, and includes primarily the furnishing of private investment capital from the United States and the supplying of technically trained experts in various fields to serve the needs of the host country.

In the course of its execution, American technicians have aided agriculture in India, mines in Myanmar, and public health in Thailand as well as many other similar projects.

Many people regard the programme as especially hopeful because of its practical application. Instead of involving intergovermental relationship at a high level, it actually represents individuals engaged in extending a helping hand to other individuals in an attack upon problems that are highly personnel in their impact.

Many of the great failures of the programme have come as a result of attempts to impose an American procedure upon a situation completely unsuitable for it; likewise, its greatest successes have accompanied a realization that an agricultural problem in India, for example, may be solved only by the gradual application of Western techniques to a situation that is and will remain uniquely Indian. This of necessity has required the modification of many Western techniques of organization, efficiency, and production in order to fit them within the bounds of a differing value structure.

Other Individual Contacts

The increasing amount of individual international contact is the movement of unorganized private citizens in the pursuit of their individual interests. In the part of world which is still sufficiently free to permit reasonably easy movement buy private individuals across frontiers, there is a constant two-way traffic. The reasons for these movements are almost as numerous as there are people moving, but we may at least indicate certain major categories.

Education. International education is an old custom, especially in the Western world. Since the Middle Ages it has been normal for students to seek the completion of their formal education in foreign institutions. This, however, was largely confined to Europe, where a common culture existed of which the universities were among the principal custodians.

Thus, the movement of students remained within reasonably limited bounds. Today, however, educational interchange upon an international basis includes not only the states of the Western world but representatives of Oriental and other chapters as well.

The United States plays a leading role in this process. As a matter of policy the US government emphasizes private international contact through education, feeling that in this important area real progress can be made onwards minimizing inter cultural tension.

It operates an international educational exchange programme whereby foreign students and professors from all over the world may come to the United States to study or teach; in 1953-54 there were over 30,000 such visitors in American institutions of higher learning. The similar data in the year 2002 have reached to millions.

At the same time many-sided programme undertakes to make study broad available to American students. The largest single such group are the Fluorite scholars, Approximately 600 per year, who study in any of some nineteen states in Europe or Asia.

They enjoy scholarships provided by the unexpended accounts remaining from United States lend-lease operations during World War II. Similar opportunities exist for American professors, both to teach and to do research abroad, under the Fluorite programme.

There are many privately financed international fellowships (248 of which were awarded between 1947 and 1952), and the Ford Foundation fellowships for study in the Middle and Far East.

All in all, the programme of American campuses, even small campuses, are commonplace; Americans abroad are an equally familiar phenomenon. On the campuses of several large American universities—and in many European universities as well—are located ' International houses'.

These are residence and social centres for foreign students. In this way students from abroad not only learn about the United States, but acquire much sophistication from the intimate contact with other foreign students.

Thus an Indian student in the United States may have a

Norwegian as a room-mate. In this way the process of student acculturation gains a new dimension. Education an exchange between Europe and the Orient.

It is particularly important that the lessons of common humanity and sympathetic understanding be taught within the college and university community in all states because it is from this group that the leaders of the future will come.

The attitude toward other peoples held by the current generation of college students in the United States can never be the same as a result of its contact with so many foreign students.

When this group of college-age people have matured to the point of taking over national leadership themselves, their views and their policy cannot but reflect the conditioning toward individuals of other cultures that occurred during their student days.

Recreation and Sports. The pursuit of recreation leads many individuals into international set,' which journeyed from one famous recreational playground and another, but its importance was never great and today is negligible.

Of much more significance is organized international athletic competition. The most publicized event of this sort is of course the quadrennial Olympic games, in which athletes from all over the world compete in many different events. But it would be difficult to mention a form of athletics, either professional or amateur, which does not extend into the international arena.

Team sports, such as soccer, football, basketball, baseball, water polo, and hockey have regularly scheduled international tournaments; in addition, national champions in these and other sports make international tours as a matter of course.

A noteworthy example of international athletic competition is the annual pursuit of the Davis Cup, for which national teams of tennis players compete in a world-wide elimination tournament. Individual sports—tennis, golf, boxing, wrestling, weight lifting, tract and field, and the like—also provide innumerable opportunities for international competition. Indeed, so systematized in international athletic competition that almost any athlete of sufficient talent, regardless of his particularly speciality, can look forward to the opportunity of performing in foreign land and in competition with opponents of different nationalities.

It is difficult, however, to measure the effect of this relationship upon international understanding. An example was perhaps afforded by the 1952 Olympic games in Helsinki.

The Soviet Union participated for the first time and the games were marred by ill-tempered disputes about the method of scoring points in the team completion (which was entirely unofficial; all Olympic championships are individual). Despite the Soviet government's desire to make political capital out of the competition and the unfavourable atmosphere of Russo-American relations at the time, American team members reported to the press that they found their Russian opponents to be very pleasant individuals and sturdy competitors. What the Russian athletes told their government we have no way of knowing.

Tourism. Perhaps the most prolific source of personal international experiences is tourism. Since the war American tourists and travellers have come to include the entire globe in their itinerary, taken great advantage of the growth of air transportation.

The United States government has encouraged this practice for two reasons. In the first place tourist expenditures represent a very considerable transfer of dollars into foreign hands, making it easier for them to purchase American goods. In the second, tourism, being travel for no ulterior purpose, provides an ideal opportunity for Americans to learn about the ways of life in foreign countries. As a rest tourism by Americans has grown to remarkable proportions and the American who has 'been abroad' is no longer a local curiosity throughout each of the United States.

Europeans are almost as great travellers as are Americans and, despite currency and travel restrictions, have covered much of the Western world with their wanderings.

In Asia, the smallness of the leisure class and the great distances to be traversed have made travel by Asians less common; however, much of non-communist Asia is regularly visited by tourists from the West and some international contact thus takes place.

The Effects of World War II

Hostile occupation, the forcible transfer of workers, prisoners of war, displaced persons, refugees, and military comradeship all produced mass international contacts among private persons upon a scale unmatched at any time before or since.

Its effects are still being felt. Many Frenchmen perceived, even in the bitterness of defeat, that the Germans are human beings and the most of them are human beings and that most of them are decent; Germans learned the same about the French.

The Japanese, at first despised and then hysterically hated by Americans, turned out on closer acquaintance to be human beings who have the same sort of personal problems as we do but who solve them somewhat differently. Even the Soviet Union felt the impact.

The hundreds of thousands of Red Army soldiers who saw the West with their won eyes in Germany and Austria, as well as the Russian slave labourers Hitler forcibly deported to the West during the war, will never again have the same degree of trust in the Kremlin's propaganda about the decayed and dying West.

In this way the world reaped an unexpected harvest of good from the war. The sheer volume of personal contact that developed, ranging from casual acquaintanceship to international marriages, has worked and will continue to work a fundamental change in the outlook of millions of people.

The International Sense of Community

Concept of Community. The "community" is a nebulous. There are four essential aspects of a community. First, it is composed of individuals who may or may not be organized into subgroups. Second, these individuals have extensive and habitual relations with one another which are sufficiently well organized to proceed upon a highly predictable basis. Third, there exists within the group a generally recognized moral consensus that establishes the value system in whose terms certain are demanded by the community, others encouraged or permitted, and the others prohibited. Fourth, the habitual relations of the individuals and the value system are both reflected in a framework of institutions. The people who constitute the community recognize their mutual bonds and order their behaviour accordingly.

International Community Sense. The international sense of community, therefore consists in the realization shared by an increasing number of individuals in almost all states of the world that they form part of a group which processes most of the marks of a true community.

This community bypasses political organization and political action. Its focus of emphasis is upon the rough identity of interest shared by its members in their private lives. In terms of the criteria of a communist which the international community displays the following characteristics.

Its members are generally organized into subgroups (private and public international organization), but whether within or without such a subgroup, extensive and habitual personal relations are carried on. These are developing certain procedural patterns and organization, and predictability in these relationship is developing rapidly.

To enforce its value judgments the international community is developing a set of sanctions, most of them thus far informal, to prescribe desirable behaviour and to punish antisocial conduct.

Extensive institutional elaboration of this community sense has already taken place land the process in continuing to day at the ever-increasing rate.

Nationalism and Technology. Since the creation of the nation-state system about four centuries ago, the largest political unit reflecting the sense of community shared by its members has been the national state. The state had to win its victory over other, smaller community units for the prize of the loyalty of its people.

The history of the development of the state in modern times can be told in terms of the expansion of the community sense of the people until it actually encompassed the entire national group. Two forces played critical roles in this process.

The first was the development of modern nationalism, which identified the body of citizens with the effective community; the second was modern technology which made the pretensions of nationalism a reality by making it possible for all people within a state to maintain close and habitual relations with all the others.

The political community of which most individuals feel a part today is coterminus with the keep-political group called the nation and also with the boundaries within which that nation dwells.

These two forces that share responsibility for the state-based community to operate in vastly different ways in modern context. Nationalism in most societies today however more sharp distinctions between the in-group and all out-groups, and demonstrates an increasing proclivity toward ethnocentric excesses; on the other hand, the advance of modern technology did not come to a halt at the frontiers of the national state but instead leaped over them. The technological frontier now extends to the outermost limits of the entire world. It is an easy matter for individuals to maintain `extensive relations' upon an organized basis with people in all other states.

The international-community sense is most conspicuous among those individuals everywhere who have accepted the implications of global technology and who have therefore won freedom from the more limited points of view imposed by the more restrictive variety of nationalism.

Components of the International-Community Sense

If the international-community sense is defined as an attitude shared by large numbers of individuals throughout the world, it now becomes appropriate to consider its component parts. Individuals vary in their understanding of what membership in the international community means; many persons pursue an active part in the affairs of the community without realizing the assumptions upon which they are proceeding. Yet we can formulate a reasonably clear outline of the philosophical postulates upon which the international-community sense is built.

Individualism. In the first place, the international-community sense is individualistic in its outlook. It rejects the totalitarian implications of the dogma of the modern state and denies that men have no higher destiny than to serve their governments in all ways that political leadership deems to befitting. It clearly involves an elevation of the claims of the individual to dignity and worthy over the pretensions of the state to absolute dominance.

Since in international affairs the state is everything and the individual has no legal existence, the international-community sense rejects much of international law and almost all of what we know as 'power politics.'

In other words, it is a philosophy if international affairs which centres upon the individual human being instead of upon the abstract entity of the state. In this sense it is more realistic than nationalistic particulars since the individual has objective reality and the state and the national do not.

Paradoxically, an outlook which emphasizes the prime importance of the individual should seek the broadest possible base of organization. If the state today results in the abasement of a individual, it might be thought odd to urge the creation of a new community to include of mankind; to change from a large group to one still larger in the name of more dignity and freedom for the individual is a seeming contradiction. The state form of organization, say the apologists for the international community, obstructs the most efficient use of the technological resources of the world in terms of the maximum benefit for individuals; the economies of large-scale production can be federalized by utilizing all mankind in a single body of producers and consumers.

Anti-Sadism. The international-community sense not only denies the pre-eminence of the state over the individual; its outlook is primarily non-political. Instead of being concerned with problems of national interest, national power, and national prestige, it makes a special point of the highly personal problems of individuals in the economic, social, and psychological areas. It seems to argue that although man unquestionably is a political being, he is first and always a human; as such, he is beset from birth with a host of situations that strike him much more directly than even the most fervent pleas of political authority.

He must find food and shelter; he must marry and establish a family; he must combat disease; he must gain sufficient knowledge of socially useful skills to enable him to cope with the world; he must learn the formal and informal rules of social organization so that he can fit himself meaningful into the group of which he is a part.

The international-community sense concentrates upon these aspects of the lives of individuals and seeks to discover some of the solutions to these personal problems. It elevates the private life of man over the political life, and views government as one of the possible vehicles for the enrichment and fulfilment of the life of individuals rather than than as the embodiment of the supremacy of the political virtues.

In the international field it accordingly expects from government a different role from that played by the states of today, it demands co-operative attack by political authority upon the problems of men rather than the competitive pursuit of national interest.

Individual Interest. The idea of the international community is founded upon the basic identity of interest among all individuals. Building upon the sociological and anthropological truth of essential similarity of all people and the fact that cultural and societal differences between men is learned rather than innate, the international-community sense assumes fail all men share basically the same needs and desires. From this assumption that all men want basically the same things for themselves, the next condition is that the primary business of men efficient programme of meeting as many as possible of these individual demands. Whatever in the way of governmental policy anywhere serves to improve the lot of individuals is deemed desirable; whatever serves any other purpose is held to be of secondary importance. This means that the shares of the sense of international community reject cost of the nationalist apparatus of modern international politics on the ground that it creates a false disharmony of interest between individuals of different national groups.

All these divisive forces of modern world life are real and powerful in their effect upon human emotions, and to seek to offset them by attempts at scientific refutation is a waste of time. The only way in which an individual who denies his identity of interest with all other men can be brought to change his mind is for him to be placed in situations of direct contact with representatives of alien cultures. Once brought face to face with the obvious fact that these strangers must cope with the same sort of problems as he does, the psychological underpinnings of his faith in his own uniqueness are weakened.

Once enough individuals had gained the sophistication in outlook that made it possible for them to grasp the important fact of the essential sameness of human everywhere, the concept of international community became a potent force in world affairs.

No Confidence in State Mechanism. Consequent upon the defect of technology, many men everywhere have developed doubts about the ultimate validity of political values. They wonder whether the demands that international politics make upon individuals return rewards that are worth what they cost and whether the fate of men is to remain forever divided into mutually competitive groups.

The answer to these questions is in the negative they argue that men possess the physical resources to meet the demands of modern life provided a cooperative programme undertaken in a spirit of goodwill be initiated upon a world-wide basis.

Resultantly they no longer have may confidence that the international political system, founded upon the sovereignty of the state and operating upon the principles of power and of expediency, can every produce any lasting improvement of human happiness.

Theirs, however, is not simply a theory of philosophic anarchy hoping for a day of brotherhood that will make political organization unnecessary. The advocates of the international community seek to keep their policy practice and realistic. They have no rigid formula for action except in terms, of the eventual recognition of the equal right of all individuals to a reasonably adequate satisfaction of their basic needs.

Therefore, although distrusting the nation-state and the system of world politics as presently constituted and motivated, they do not necessarily call for its outright rejection. Some set a system of world government as the only possible solution, but most content themselves with urging joint socio-economic policy at an international level upon the governments of the present-day world. For many people, the doubt about the personal rewards derived from state-centred international politics has not yet matured into recognition and an acceptance of the international community.

They are disillusioned about the future of men under the nation-state system, but are unable to make the transfer of allegiance to a broader basis of identification.

Nationalism, cultural isolationism, and the pressures of ideologies furnish too great an emotional obstacle for them to overcome.

A Programme of Action. A remarkable feature of a person who shares the international community sense is his dedication to a programme of action in its behalf.

In fact, individuals vary in the exten. of their commitment in this regard as well as in the kind and extent of specific actions they undertake, but so many are the problems to be solved and so compelling is felt to be the need for their solution that purposeful activity on behalf of the goals of the community is a constant characteristic of one who feels himself a part of it.

Most of the private international organizations, being highly specialized, accomplish comparatively little except in the area of their particular interest; many of them seem quite remote from the subject of world peace. Yet in the aggregate their impact is great.

Mention may also be made of the vast number of individuals who, with in benefit of organizational support and completely upon their own, carry of the work of the international community within the scope of their own private lives.

The total effect of thousand of such persons carrying on their programmes of agitation, education, and action over a period of years cannot leap but make a real impression upon the consciousness of governments anywhere.

Consequently, individuals interested in the advancement of the international community have banded into pressure groups in order to stimulate governmental action in that direction.

The steps taken by governments in this field include the creation and operation of special-purpose international organizations, the furthering of the social and economic work of the United Nations, and the initiation of maltreat policies of relief and rehabilitation of individuals in other states (outstanding examples are the **Point IV** programme of the United States and the **Colombo Plan** of the British Commonwealth).

It cannot be denied, however that governments often have mixed motives in their operations in this field; some of them have a direct national interest in the development of a real international community sense and co-operate much more willingly than do others whose policy is founded upon a perpetuation of the national differences that divide mankind. In almost every instance, the effective implementation of any such governmental policy necessitates the unremitting application of pressure by individuals and groups who subscribe to the policy themselves to the point of becoming political activists in its support.

Private International Organizations

A private international organization is composed of private persons who band together upon an international basis either for the direct accomplishment of an end they have in common or else to bring pressure upon their respective governments to initiate policy in harmony with their objectives.

There are over 700 such organisations in existence at the present time, with a bewildering variety of stated purposes. They belong to either the figurative type, being composed of a number of suborganizations set up upon a national basis, or else to the consolidated type, which is truly international with no organizational apparatus intervening between the individual member and the leadership of the entire group.

The most important of them have certain structural features in common. They all have a central headquarters under the direction of a chief executive officer who normally serves as spokesman for the organization, together with some form of regularly scheduled conference of the entire membership at their representatives, at which general policy is made for the organization.

(1) *Economic Organisations.* Perhaps the largest category of private international organizations is furnished by those whose objectives are the economic betterment of the individual members. At least three major sub classifications can be discerned. Manufacturing and trade organizations include perhaps the most influential single private international organization, the International Chamber of Commerce.

Other typical types are the International Carriage and Van Union, the International Fiscal Association, the International Federation of Newspaper Publishers and Editors and the International Union of Architects. Labour organizations include the three most powerful international labour groups: the International Confederation of Pert Trade Unions, the World Federation of Trade Unions, and the International Federation of

Christian Trade Unions. Agricultural organizations include the International Federation of Agricultural Producers and various regional bodies.

(2) *Political Organisations.* Private international organizations with a political orientation are of two different types: they are composed either of governmental officials from various states with common problems who consult together for the more efficient accomplishment of their mission, or else of private citizens whose major function is the dissemination of information and the bringing of pressure upon their respective home governments.

The first type, composed of similarly situated government officials of various states, includes the most important of this entire category, the Inter-Parliamentary Union, whose membership is made up of legislators from many states.

Few more examples are the International City Managers' Association, the International Federation of Unions of Employees in Public and Civil Services, the International Institute of Administrative Sciences, the International Institute of Public Finance, and the International Institute of Public Law.

Pressure and propaganda organizations include the World Federation of United Nations Associations, the International Federation for Housing and Town-Planning, the International League for the Rights of Man, and the International Union of Socialist Youth. Almost all private international organizations have a pressure-propaganda aspect as part of their programme, but those given above are some for which it is the principal function.

(3) *Religious Organisations.* Religious organizations upon an international basis are numerous, representing most of the organized faith of the Western World. The Salvation Army, the World Jewish Congress, the Young Christian Workers, Pax-Romans (a Roman Catholic organization for intellectual and Cultural Affairs), the Commission of the Churches on International Affairs, the Catholic International Union for Social Service, and the Friends' World Committee are only a few of a long list.

(4) *Social Organisations.* Almost as numerous as the international organizations with an economic orientation are those whose purposes may be classified generally is social betterment. Their purposes range from the suppression of the slave rats to the fostering of temperance, including the improvement of social rift welfare activities (care for cripples, dependent children, and the incise) and the improvement of health and sanitation. Representative organizations are the International Committee of the Red Cross, the International Conference of Social Work, the International Council of women, the International Society for the Welfare of Cripples, the International Temperance Union and those two familiar ones, the World's Alliance of Young Men's Christian Associations and the world's Young women's Christian Association.

(5) *Technical and Scholarly.* Technical and specialized organizations exist in most of the fields of advanced learning. The International Statistical Institute, the International Society of Criminology, the International Political Science. Association, the International Law Association are to cite.

In all of them the purpose is the exchange of information and experiences upon an organized basis for the improvement of the technical competence of all concerned.

There remain still many other private international organizations that do not fit into any of these five categories, but the listing does at least suggest something of the scope of human activity that is affected by these bodies.

Consultation with the United Nations. Following a practice originally formalized by the League of Nations, Article 71 of the Charter of the United Nations provides for establishment of consultative relationships between private (non-governmental) organizations and the Economic and Social Council for the purposes of mutually considering problems of common interest. The Council has prepared and keeps on file a register of such organizations, which maintain a consultative relationship.

They are divided into three categories: category 'A' includes 'organizations which are closely linked with the economic or social life of the areas which they represent'; a third category includes organisations that maintain less formal relations with the Council but are available upon an ad hoc basis for consolation when such action is indicated.

By the end of 1953, there,were nine organizations in category ' A' 92 in category '›B' and 115 international groups were on the register for ad hoc consultations. The following nine organizations formed category ' A':

International Chamber of Commerce

International Confederation of Free Trade Unions

International Cooperative Alliance

International Federation of Agricultural Producers

International Federation of Christian Trade Unions

International Organization of Employers

Inter-Parliamentary Union

World Federation of Trade Unions

World Federation of United Nations Associations

Public International Unions

These are international organizations whose orientation and purposes are clearly toward the individual.

Since they are governmental, they operate upon a more formal basis than do the private groups and as a result both gain and lose in effectiveness. Their internal organisation, their membership, and their functions very so greatly that beyond certain general statements it is impossible to classify them in any meaningful fashion.

All have some kind of central bureau with permanent administrators, and provision is always made for periodic conferences; beyond that, each one organizes itself largely in terms of the international instrument which created it.

The public international organizations of specialized purposes can be divided into two groups. The first consists of those more important ones with (to quote the Charter of the United Nations) ' wide international responsibilities' which have been brought into relationship with the United Nations and are known as the specialized agencies.'

The second includes all the remainder—several hundreds of varying size and degree of formalization—which are either geographically or functionally so specialized as lent to merit relationship with the United Nations. For our purposes it will perhaps be preferable to consider the second group first.

Independent Public International Unions

1. *Transportation and Communication, and Economics.* Since the organization and structure of these bodies differ so widely, the only possible way to summarize their operations is in terms of the functions to which they address themselves.

The inter-American Coffee Board deals with the orderly marketing of coffee, the International Tin Committee with tin, and the now defunct Sugar Union. With sugar Agricultural organizations likewise exist, but most of their functions have been merged with the Food and Agricultural Organizations, one of the specialized agencies of the United Nations.

Perhaps the most impressive example of how far states will go in creating cards to deal with economic matters is furnished by the European Coal and Steel Community, the formal institution executing the Schuman Plan for the pooling of the coal and steel industry of the six western European sues of France, West Germany, Italy, Belgium, Luxembourg, and the Netherlands.

2. *Social, Cultural, and Scientific.* Many international unions deal with social questions similar to those dealt with by the private organizations considered in the preceding section. Although many of these unions have been absorbed by various of the commissions and specialized agencies of the United Nations, a number of them still retain their autonomy and operate with reduced scope in limited areas.

Other international unions deal with cultural and scientific purposes. Such basic data as weights and measures and a standard map of the world are in the care of the International Bureau of Weights and Measures and the Central Bureau of the International Map of the World.

The International Hydrographic Bureau co-ordinates and makes available to everyone the work of the various national states in the areas of hydrograph and navigation.

United Nations Agencies

The United Nations system includes two types of organizations that deal with questions within the particular interest of the international community: first, the commission, committees, and 'special bodies' that are an integral part of the United Nations itself; second, the 'specialized agencies' that exist as independent international organizations but are 'in relationship' with the parent body.

The Economic and Social Council of the United Nations is charged with directing the activities of the first type and of 'Co-ordinating' the work of the second.

Commissions and other United Nations Agencies. The membership of the first type of agency consists of members of the United Nations appointed to the respective bodies by action of the General Assembly. Most of these bodies have names and functions that are self-explanatory.

The first type is the functional commission. These are created to deal with a particular subject, presumably of general interest to all members. A listing of the objects with which these commissions deal illustrate the scope of United Nations activity in economic and social affairs. Commissions only on the following topics; economics and employment, transportation and status of women, narcotic drugs, fiscal questions, and population question. Each of these bodies deals with its problem by making recommendations the Economic and Social Council and to the General Assembly.

A second type, economic in scope and geographic in scope and geographic in organization, is the regional commission. Three of these exist at present: the Economic Commission for Europe

(ECE), the Economic Commission for Asia and the Far East (ECAFE), and the Economic Commission for Latin America (ECLA) Membership is drawn from the states in each region and other nations with particular interest. Their action is principally co-ordinating and expending.

Procedural matters are the principal concern of standing committees. Two typical examples are the committee on Negotiations with Inter-Governmental Agencies (public international unions) and the Committee for Causation with Non-Governmental Organizations (private international organizations).

Less important are the too remaining types, the ad hoc committees and the special bodies. The first group are temporary bodies to deal with the recurrent problems for limited times; examples include the Commission on Genocide and the United Nations Appeal for Children.

The second type consists of semi-permanent administrative agencies that exercise supervisory of co-ordinating functions over particular problems.

Two of the best known of these are the Permanent Central Opium Board, which supervises the International Narcotics Trade, and the United Nations International Checked Emergency Fund (UNICEF).

The Specialized Agencies. The specialized agencies of the United Nations are separate international organizations, each created by a multilateral international agreement. Each maintains its own membership, its own bodies and administrative staff, and its own area of operations.

As a result of a special agreement between each of them and the United Nations, a chew working relationship involving co-ordination, consultation, and mutual assistance exists between the parent organization and all the spectacled agencies and between the specialized agencies themselves.

1. **The International Labour Organization** (ILO) was established in 1919 and came into relationship with the United Nations in 1946. Seventy-nine state

constitute the membership headquarters are maintained in Genre Switzerland, with branch offices throughout the world.

It operates upon it annual budget (in 1954) of 6,311,000 U.S. dollars its purposes can be summarized as the improvement of the condition of labour throughout the world and the removal of grave disparities among the labour forces of various station to press has been considered and it is recognized as one of the most powerful of these bodies.

2. **The Food and Agriculture Organization** of the United Nations (FAO) actually came into being in 1954 and was brought into relationship with the United Nations the following year. Seventy-one states formed the membership in 1954; headquarters are maintained at Rome.

   Its annual budget is cut over six million dollars. Its general purpose is the improvement of the comfort of living of individuals everywhere by obtaining more efficient intention and distribution of food and agricultural products.

   Although multicapped buy the refusal of the Communist bloc to accept membership by theorize that food is a political weapon and should be dealt with accordingly, it has had some success in its mission.

3. **The United Nations Educational, Scientific, and Cultural Organization** (UNESCO) was created late in 1946 and entered into its United Nations relationship several weeks later in the same year.

   Seventy-two states are members (the USSR, the Ukraine, and Bgelorussia joined during 1954) and turn 60 national commissions now exist to execute the work within the member states, headquarters are in Paris. The annual budget is over nine million dollars.

   The preamble to the UNESCO constitution contains

the famous statement that since wars begin in the minds of men, it is in the minds of men that the defenses of peace must be constructed.

The organization seeks to attain this end though active promotion of the international exchange of education, scientific, and cultural information. Its work has been provocative of carryovers in many states, including the United States; however, its approach is felt by many to be potentially valuable in the development of the international-community sense.

4. **The International Civil Aviation Organization** (ICAO) began its existent in 1947 and almost immediately entered into a relationship with the United Nations. Sixty-three states maintain memberships headquarters of the organization are in Montreal.

   Branch offices are maintained in Paris, Lima, Cairo, and Melbourne. The annual budget is just over three million Canada dollars. The scope of the organization's concern includes the whole of civil aviation, with emphasis on the rapid and orderly extension of civilization facilities throughout the world.

5. **The International Bank for Reconstruction and Development** (IBRD) came into being late in 1945 and entered into relationship with the United Nations two years later. Fifty-seven countries maintain membership; arrival other applications are pending. Headquarters are located in Washington, with a European office in Paris.

   The Bank is capitalized at approximately billion dollars, of which 20 per cent is available for the making of loans; of administrative budget runs in the neighbourhood of five million dollars. The purpose of the Bank is indicated in its name; it exists as a lending and guaranteeing agency to providing financing for Governments to undertake erects of reconstructions development.

6. **The International Monetary Fund** (IMF) has the same dates of cooption and of adherence to the United Nations as does the Bank, its organization. The same 57 states that form the membership of the Bank to constitute the membership of the fund. Its headquarters are in Washington in the same building that houses the Bank.

   The Fund provides approximately eight billion dollars to be used in stabilizing the currency of the membership in the progressive elimination of exchange limitations and restrictions of the kinds, and in the liberation of world trade.

7. **The World Health Organization** (WHO), which was preceded by several temporary bodies after the war, officially went into operation in 1947 and almost immediately established its relationship with the United Nations. The WHO has one of largest memberships of all the specialized agencies of 81 states, plus three associate members.

   Headquarters are in Geneva and nine regional offices are maintained. Its budget is somewhat more externship than some of the others—nine million dollars. Its objective is 'the attained by all people of the highest possible level of health'.

   The following is a brief list of the categories of its operations: control of communicable diseases, maternal and child health, environmental sanitation, mental health, social and occupational health, nutrition, public-health education, nursing, co-ordination of research, epidemiological service, health statistics, biological standardization, antibiotics, and narcotics. It co-operates actively with national governments, with private organizations, and with other international bodies, and carries on much work of its own, including an extensive programme of publication.

8. **The Original Postal Union** (UPU) was created in 1874; in 1948 its constitution was amended to incorporate an agreement bringing it into relationship with the United Nations. The UPU is the closest approximation to a truly universal international organization. Its membership totals 93, which includes all of the civilized and semi-civilized states of the world. Its headquarters are in Berne, Switzerland.

   The budget in 1954 was one and a half million Swiss France. The objective of the organization is the execution of the Berne Treaty of 1874, which lay down the principal that the signatories of the treaty form ' a single postal territory for the reciprocal exchange of correspondence.' The organization has the major functions of administering the treaty, of handling complaints, and of creating new regulations to cope with the changing conditions of postal exchange.

9. **The International Refugee Organization** (IRO) was created officially in 1948 and came into relationship with the United Nations at the same time; it terminated its operations and ended its existence in January 1952.

   Eighteen states constituted its membership at the end of its existence. Headquarters were in Geneva. Its budget was quite high because of the type of Potation it was engaged in: during the 19 months from July 1950 through January 1952, its total expenditure was nearly 400 million dollars. Its pursed was implied in its name: caring for, resettling or repatriating, and transporting the hundreds of thousands of refugees made homeless as a result of World War II.

   Its scale of operation was global, extending wherever signification bodies of refugees were gathered: Germany, Italy, Trieste, Korea, the Philippines, China and several other critical spots. The reduction of the Refugee problem to manageable proportions and the resistance of the communist states to its work caused its dissolution.

10. **The International Telecommunications Union** (ITU) grew out of coder international agreements upon telegraphy and radiotelegraphy prior a World War II. The ITU was actually created in 1934 but was reorganized at trims of a new convention in 1947.

    The new ITU formally entered into existence in 1949 and the agreement with the United Nations came into force at the same time. Ninety countries and territories have joined; headquarters are in Geneva.

    The budget is in the neighbourhood of six million quarters are Frances. The organization aims at the more efficient and effective use of the devices of international telecommunication.

    It assigns radio frequencies to members, attempts to maintain rates for telecommunication services at as by a rate as possible, and makes studies and formulates recommendations to wall members on telecommunication subjects.

11. The **World Meteorological Organization** (WMO) grew out of the International Meteorological Organization that was founded in 1878. The WMO was formally established in 1951. The membership is made up of 58 states and 24 territories, a total of 82. Headquarters are in Geneva; regional offices are maintained in six areas of the world.

    The annual budget for 1954 was $363,000. Its purposes include co-ordination and supervising the gathering and exchange of weather information and application of the science of metrology to all forms of human activity. These are the Inter-Governmental Maritime Consultative Organization (IMCO) and the International Trade Organization (ITO). Each waits the day when enough states ratify the respective conventions for it to go into operation.

The purposes of IMCO are clear from its name. ITO was provided for in 1948 at a meeting in Havana, where a Charter was drawn. The reduction of tariffs upon a world-wide scale, clearly implied by the Havana Charter, has aroused much resistance in many states and rectifications have been slow.

In the meantime, an Interim Commission for ITO has been occupied mainly in securing the implementation of the General Agreement for Tariffs and Trade (GATT), which was entered into in 1947 and provides for bilateral negotiations between the signatories in the direction of tariff reductions.

What do all these institutions, organizations, and agencies mean with the guard to the status of the international community? They represent a right accumulation of organized effort by individuals, groups, and governments upon the common social and economic problems of men.

The good number of members of the various specialized agencies of the United Nations into Cates accurately how widespread throughout the world in public interest in what we have termed the international community.

The majority of the state of the world have demonstrated the insistence of their peoples that concrete action be taken in the direction of solving some of the continuing problems of individual life in a world grown more complex and insecure.

World Politics and the international community

In considering the implications for world politics of the existence of the international community and its progressive realization, we must first recognize the constant conflict that is inherent in the relations of the nation-state with the international community.

To the extent that an individual adheres to the international community his nationalist identification is weakened. It is because this dichotomy is so clear in contemporary world affairs that the advance and the development of the international community is fought so bitterly by chauvinists in every state.

Some governments in the world are the therewhose national interest leads them to foster the growth of international institutions of a community nature, but they are and promise to be for a long time in the minority.

Advantages of the state. In the struggle for individual loyalty that is going on between the state and the international community, it is self-evident that the state enjoys certain advantages. There are a least three reasons which help explain this situation.

The state is universal in its appeal and comes before individuals at every turn in their lives. The international community, on the other hand, presents itself to most people only in terms of a single interest or a small group of them. Merely in terms of the number of appeals aimed at individuals, the state makes contact with its citizens many more times and upon many more issues than does the community. A case can, of course, be made for the universality of the international community, but the great majority of men, if they are aware of the community at all, think of it in terms only of the one or two ways in witch it impinges upon them directly. A second appeal of the state is emotional.

For most individuals the international community is defected upon rational grounds involving a logical and dispassionate judgment of the relative merits of the two systems. In a conflict for loyalty by seen emotional and rational appeals, the former enjoys most of the advantages. There are individuals whose attachment to the concept of the community is as emotional as is the sense of nationalist dedication of most other people, but thus far they constitute only a relative handful.

So long as governments can evoke mass emotional reactions to the manipulation of nationalist stimuli, the rate of growth of the international community will continue to be slow.

Thirdly, the state can command the obedience of its citizens in a way at present barred to the community: the reliance upon coercion. The state may compel agreement, or at least the absence of open dissent; the only adherents the community has are those who become so through voluntary action. Governments in many states have undertaken deliberate policies with the object of obstructing the growth of community institutions upon as international level and to destroying the sense of international community.

Reasons for the Growth of the Community Sense. Why has the community sense continued to attract more supporters at the very same time that the intensity of international conflict has increased?

It has become obvious from the foregoing discussion that increasing individual contact has broadened the comprehension of the outside world by individuals, and that co-operative action has been forced from states as a result.

Probably, the important single factor in the growth of the international-community sense however has been the widespread revulsion of individuals against the perpetuation of a system that has brought two catastrophic wars in a generation and constantly threatens to produce a third.

Men have placed themselves at the service of their states for generations; now, with the technology of mass destruction having become an exact science many of them are becoming unwilling to go on. In this attitude there is no element of either cowardice or disloyalty; the way of competition, crisis, and conflict, they seem to say, has brought only ruin and stalemate. Mankind is instead of seeking positive attack upon international problems incorporating agreement and good faith.

As governments today require mass support from pupulations in order to achieve even minimal ends in world politics, statesmen have been object to pay grudging respect to this mass attitude. Even the Soviet leadership whatever its ultimate intentions, has found it necessary constantly to read sure its own people that peace is its only objective.

6

World Politics: The Future

The contemporary society is no more at a watershed of history than were many previous generations, and our role may not be original with us; other ages have been faced with equally grave responsibilities. Nevertheless, whether ours is a uniquely perplexed destiny or merely one shared by our ancestors, the choices that have fallen to us are both difficult and important. What we decide now will affect the world for decades to come.

Our vision is, of course, limited; we shall not be able accurately to predict details of the course of events during the next phase or the history of international relations. At the very least, however, we may take an overall view of the range of possibilities of the future, examine the good and bad portents, and review some of the unsolved problem with which we may expect to grapple in the years to come. In this way we may be able to gain some insight into the dimensions of the task facing mankind and perhaps gather a few clues how to proceed.

The Prospects

The alternatives, using what logic we can apply to a situation and a system which we have learned to be fundamentally illogical, we may postulate initially that the future of the world political system either will be marked by change or by stability. If change occurs it will be either destructive or constructive; furthermore, the pace of either type of change may be rapid, or it may be more gradual and evolutionary. In this way, we arrive at five possible alternative routes which the future of world politics and the state system might take, depending on both the direction and the speed it assumes: (1) complete and sudden destruction; (2) gradual deterioration, marked by progressively greater inability to solve problems and meet challenges; (3) a continuation of the present system with no great change—the middle course; (4) problems; (5) rapid and radical transformation into different and much better system.

Relative Probabilities

Destruction and Transformation. Which of these alternative developments is most likely to occur? Admitting that all five are theoretically and perhaps practically possible, can we pick out certain of them as being more likely to take place than others? It is perhaps safest to start by relegating both extremes—the first and the last in the list above—to the category of the least possible. Rapid destruction of society or its equally rapid transformation is possible in any period of history, and instances of the occurrence of each can be found. In any situation, however, sudden and extreme institutional and social change is usually the least probable outcome; man seems to prefer other, less drastic solutions to his problems. Certainly it must be admitted that today we possess the technical knowledge either to wipe out civilization and perhaps humanity or to reorganize society on a basis of abundance for all. Human will, rather than the limits on human intellect, holds us back from accepting either of these courses. While recognizing as always that judgments about the future behaviour of men are inevitably subjective, we may nonetheless conclude at this point that it is relatively unlikely that either total catastrophe or total renaissance will mark the future of international politics.

Deterioration or Evolution: This evolution may result in a multiplying frustration as the system proves more and more incapable of satisfying the demands placed upon it, or it may culminate in a gradual overhaul and revision of the structure of international society and the successful resolution of issues that presently defy attack.

Trend to Frustration. Among the various factors to be noted: the rigidity of the world political structure, marked by bipolarity and the inability to compromise meaningfully; the intensity of nationalism and nationalist conflict, which leads to the rejection of all solutions to problems except absolute ones; the present failure to control the trend toward bigger and more deadly weapons and techniques of destruction; and the fact that so many basic problems of human life over reach state boundaries and hence do not permit of easy solution in a state-centred world.

To cite, these are only a few of the conditions that combine to create a slowly growing impression that the fundamental problems of international life are, and will continue to be, insoluble. If this attitude should become the prevailing one in the minds of men, the resultant atmosphere of frustration and defeat would lines capably spell the ultimate failure and collapse of international relations.

We cannot foretell what would replace the present system but that it would be vastly different and of no guaranteed greater effectiveness we may be sure.

The deterioration and collapse of the present framework of world affairs must be admitted to be genuine possibility. It would require only the projection and intensification of trends already present to become a reality.

Constructive evolution. On the other hand, possibilities of constructive evolution in international affairs are also present in the contemporary scene, and forces are at work which give us at least as much reason to hope for final success as to fear final defeat.

There are grounds enough for a restrained optimism, or at least enough to discourage an unrelieved pessimism. In the main, they reflect attempts to escape from the more oppressive consequences of the inability of the state system to meet the demands placed upon it.

They combine to furnish real evidence that the controlling trend of the future of world politics might be a reasonably happy one, or at least that the negative omens can be balanced by positive ones.

We have already discussed the evolving sense of international community, which is the first of the favourable factors. It would be unrealistic in the extreme to claim that this particular attitude is dominant in world affairs today or that it will become so relatively soon.

It would be inaccurate to deny that the international-community sense exists and that it is exerting a perceptible influence on the course of events. There is also some basis for feeling that this sentiment is on the increase and that it will be even more influential in the future as something of a counterweight to the divisive and potentially upsetting force of nationalism.

It takes its expression most frequently in the form of supranational consensus and an emerging world public opinion. A favourable sign in world politics is the growing caution of statesmen. Although the conditions that produce breakdown and war are ever present, it is clear that policy makers in all major states are less willing today to run the risk of being responsible for total disaster.

Caution on the part of national leaders provides time for the nations to work out alternatives, time to allow heated passions to cool, time to develop bases for understanding—more time, perhaps, than some pessimistic observers have been willing to grant mankind. If statesmen continue to recoil from the possibility of putting civilization to the final awful test, the prospects for progress and the discovery of adequate techniques of operation on an international level will be brighter.

The final ground for hope grows out of the first two: the growing trend toward the creation of new international and supra-national agencies to deal with new problems. It seems obvious that new situations call for new approaches, and that part of the failure of contemporary international society to resolve the crises of our age is due to the inadequacy of available techniques.

The shortcomings of the present state system are not difficult to discover and we have made much of them in this volume;

the system is not without its real advantages, however. Not the least of these is its familiarity.

Modern civilized man is at home in the state and feels in harmony with his environment when he is accomplishing the traditional purposes of national interest in the time-honoured way.

Among the other reasons for the probable survival of the present system are the monopoly of power exercised by the state form over individuals and the compelling emotional attachment felt by most of us for the traditions and goals of nationalism.

If one accepts as a working hypothesis the idea the international relations will continue in the future much as the past, this does not rule out of the picture the possibility of change, even of substantial change.

The forces of deterioration and evolution considered above are real and powerful, and even if they do not become dominant they will materially affect the day-by-day course of international politics.

Indeed, it is not difficult to envisage the nation-state system of the future functioning according to the same principles as energize it today, but at the same time being affected by (and affecting) the twin forces of deterioration and evolution.

Perhaps the international scene of the next generation or two will be the final battleground between these historic trends; out of such a struggle would come the decision on the ultimate direction in which civilization will move.

More likely the struggle between stagnation and change will take place within the state system and, as in the present era, the tide of battle will ebb and flow. For a time progress might be in the ascendant and impose its will upon the system; then reaction would set in and frustration would again become the order of the day, to be later replaced by a new era of progress as the cycle begins again.

In many ways this alternative seems the most probable of all; one is always on scientifically sounder ground in predicting limited social change and the perpetuation of institutions than in forecasting upheavals and revolutions. Nevertheless, in good conscience we cannot rule out the possibility that one or the other of the extreme roads mentioned earlier may be the one chosen.

International explosion is always possible; less likely, but also conceivable, is a sudden voluntary transformation of the system. The first is so terrifying to contemplate, however, and the second so difficult of achievement, that either radical outcome is relatively unlikely.

Somewhere between the steady and uninterrupted deterioration into complete frustration and the continued smooth evolution toward a new and better system lies the more probable future course of world politics.

Issues of the Future

No tabulation of the pressing issues with which international society will have to deal in the future can be much more than a reflection of the interests and prejudices of its compiler. We have already learned that international problems grow out of specific historical contexts and that accident and chance play a significant part in the determination of the crises of any particular age.

None of us can be certain of the next twist of fate that will presents us with another perplexing decision. The most we can do it to attain the best possible understanding of the present in order to be better prepared for the eventualities of the future. It would therefore be unwise to make a list of current issues and to imply that their solution would insure a smooth and satisfying future.

Nevertheless, it is possible to enumerate some of the problems of the present day which promise to continue unsolved into the immediate future and perhaps into the long-range future as well.

In the three preceding chapters we examined a number of specific problem areas of current international politics. Here we shall phrase the issues in somewhat different terms. The political, economic, and psychological problems we considered earlier are examples of questions that grow out of particular conditions of time place, and participants. They are, in other words, truly contemporary.

The smaller number we shall briefly analyze in this section are inherent in the present structure of world affairs and are to a great extent independent of time or place. They give evidence of being at least semi-permanent; it is probable that they will continue to plague later generations despite possible major changes in their geographic, psychological, or material bases.

Because of their fundamental and enduring character, we may assume that their future importance will be at least as great as their present significance.

In this chapter we shall consider five such basic issues. They are not listed in any order of importance; rather, since they are so interconnected, it would be logical to consider them as being of equal pertinence. The five chosen for consideration here are the issue of war; the issue of communism; the issue of Asia; the issue of atomic energy; and energy; and the issue of international organization.

The Issue of War

None of us needs to be reminded of the impact that the prospect of war has had one our lives, in an age when anxiety is endemic this fear of a new war may well be the most powerful of our insecurities.

Much of the climate of international politics today is the result of a ear-hysterical search by government for some insulation against their being engulfed in another holocaust which might return men to the dark Ages.

It seems clear that little respite will be granted us in the future from this continuing anger and that we shall have to wrestle with the problem of war for long years to come.

What can we say at the present time to throw this issue into some sort of perspective?

We have come upon the institution of war at every turn of our analysis of international affairs. We have examined its place as the only final determinant of international disagreements, we have considered different technique and philosophies of warfare, we have studied its incidence and its prospects in the contemporary world.

We have concluded that war is a 'normal' aspect of international affairs and that to abolish the institution would necessitate a complete reconstitution of international society.

If man is unwilling or unable to undertake such as thoroughgoing renovation of the methodology of international affairs, he must perforce prepare himself to live permanently with the knowledge that an outbreak of mass hostilities always possible and, furthermore, that such a conflict would involve the new dimensions of destruction brought into being by an ever-expanding technology.

Under these conditions, it would appear that a reconsideration of some of the implications of war would be of some help.

What Can be Won by War? Perhaps the first concern should be to remind over selves of what can be won by means of war. We need to keep in mind that war as an instrument of policy in the nation-state system is subject to serious limitations.

Certain objectives, for example, are forever beyond its reach. It cannot convince defeated enemy of its moral blindness and inherent unworthiness; it cannot win friendship, nor can it extirpate hatred. If war must be lived with, it should be confined to such purposes as it can efficiently accomplish.

This is particularly true when we consider total war. This type of struggle, with its objectives of absolute destruction, is feasible only when such goals are truly dictated by national interest.

To unleash such engines of mass destruction as the hydrogen

bomb in pursuit of an unattainable objective or a frivolous one would be to justify the most extravagant prophecies of the doom of civilization. Only by being aware of what can be gained by war—and, equally important, what cannot be gained by it-can we maintain our existence under the present system.

Will We Pay the Price for Peace? Very few, if any, humans can honestly say that they prefer war as a method of existence to peace. Almost all of us as individuals would prefer war as a method of existence to peace. Almost all of us as individuals would prefer to live out our lives in relative harmony with our neighbours, settling such disputes as may arise by non-violent means.

It is usually as political beings, as citizens of a state and members of a nation, that we become belligerent.

If war is such an undesirable condition among states, it must follow that peace is preferable. What is not so clear is whether we shall be willing to pay the price for peace.

Peace can be maintained, even in the nation-state system, if the will to do so is present. The avoidance of war requires that at least three principles be active in the foreign policy of every state.

These 'rules of peace' might be phrased as follows: (1) never get into a situation where war is inevitable; (2) use all alternative methods of settling disputes; (3) accept less than total victory in any situation.

If states were to embody these ideas in their relations with one another, the maintenance of peace on a reasonable basis of stability would be a much easier task than it is at present.

We must admit that it would be difficult to persuade the people of any powerful state to accept these ideas and the foreign policy they necessitate; to gain adherence by all major states would be a truly formidable task.

Some such concept, however, would seem to be the real price for peace, and in no other way can the worst effect of the institution of war be escaped.

Can War Be Limited? Another question arise out of the experience of the past few years, when a number of small wars have been settled inconclusively without being permitted to spread major configurations. Can war be limited?

The war that frightens us is total war, and if some technique could be developed for confining small conflicts, much of the horror and uncertainty of contemporary world politics would be lessened.

Of course, the answer to the question—as we asked it—is an affirmative one; we have already seen that that statesmen can limit hostilities as regards participants and locale. What are really asking, however, is whether we shall be willing to limit war. Will we agree to suffer occasional tactical defeats in special situations in order to gain our strategic goal of peace?

If agree that war can and should be limited so long as it cannot certainly be eliminated, major policy revisions must be undertaken by all states in order to realize that goal.

We must recognize the inexpediency of objectives that can be attained only by major war and plan to employ only such forms of national power as can be successfully committed without risking total hostilities.

We must reorganize our thinking so as to recognize the grounds for possible compromise and the practical steps necessary to realize such agreements.

These, too, are bitter pills for tender nationalisms to swallow, but the alternative is clear: if the world is unwilling to limit war, it must face the consequences that will follow total war.

These, then, are some of the implications of the problem of war in the future. Since war is a thoroughly normal phenomenon in the nation-state system, it is essential to discover a basis for survival within the system.

We should consider the possibilities for confining and limiting war as regards purposes, goals, and techniques.

If the questions we have asked can be satisfactory answered, perhaps the whole problem could be reduced to manageable proportions. If they cannot, future generations may face the crises of total war in a vastly accentuated degree.

The Issue of Communism

The second problem with which the world of the future will almost certainly have to deal is that of communism. This sinister ideology, which in forty years has grown from minuscule beginnings to the most formidable threat to freedom in the world today, presents men of good will everywhere with hard choices and difficult courses of action.

Its significance shows no signs of abating, and ultimately some definite policy will have to be adopted toward it. It does not appear as if the present generation of leaders has yet discovered a formula that tells us how to deal with communism, and the resolution of the problem in any final way belongs to the future.

It is possible at this time, however, to review certain facets of the problem of communism without pretending to offer a final diagnosis or suggesting any precise course of action.

What is the Communist Problem? Fundamentally, communism is an ideology. As such, however, it existed for more than a century without becoming a major political force. It is only since the belief system became clothed with political power that it has developed into an international factor of the first order of importance.

To seek to attack communist ideas without reference to their political manifestations is pointless. The communist problem does not centre around the truth or falsity of Marxist dialectic and the doctrine of the decline of capitalism; it gains its significance from the fact that organized political bodies professing these doctrines make up a large part of the world political scene. These states constitute a pressing problem that calls for decision and action.

Viewed in these terms, the communist problem has three forms. Initially, it is an organized plan of political expansion centering in the Soviet Union and executed on the traditional stage of international politics (although involving several novel techniques).

Secondly, it is a programme of domestic subversion and revolution in which the crucial struggles take place within all non-communist states.

Third, it is the current form of the historically familiar trend to totalitarianism and authoritarianism, which has assumed different guises in different periods but always seeks to extinguish human liberty and to destroy the concept of the innate dignity of man.

In all three forms, communism presents a continuing challenge to states that seek to establish an international order of peace and stability based on individual self-realization. On all three.

Why has Communism Grown? How can we explain the growth of communism from its humble beginning to its present awesome dimensions? As late as 1945, there was only one communist state in the world; why, then, has the ideology become such a grave danger to freedom in such a short time? There are three possible reasons, each explaining apart of communist success.

In the first place, it has capitalized on political weakness. It has become foregone conclusion that whenever a 'soft spot' develops in the postwar world communist influence and Soviet power will seek to exploit such weakness. Any state unsure of its policy or its power can expect to be made an early object of communist pressure.

Second, it has exploited human misery and social maladjustment. It has played on the unquestioned injustices of the world and capitalized on the widespread desire for a more equitable distribution of the rewards of modern society. The communist movement has been alert to seize upon any delay on the part of the free world to deal effectively with international problems created by internal tension. It has been able to twist sincere social protect into mass revolution.

Finally, communism owes much of its success to the contemporary decline in the vigour of democratic belief and practice. Totalitarianism and authoritarianism has always stood ready to ensnare man whenever he has lost his faith in his own capacity for government.

Today, when so many societies are shaken by doubt and dissension communism has had very fertile soil in which to grow. In summary, then, we see that the growth of communism in recent years is due not to any major change in the doctrine itself but rather to opportunities presented it by the failure of the free world to meet its challenges.

What can we Do About Communism? Communism is a many-sided phenomenon and must be fought on all fronts where it seeks to advance. Some possible avenues of counteraction immediately suggest themselves on the basis on the foregoing analysis of the problem. Military force can be used to resist the plan of communist expansion. In many situation armed might is the only appropriate technique for dealing with the threat, but we must remain aware of the inherent limits on its utility.

Second, we must undermine the communist appeal to the discontented by providing answers to vital social questions and at the same time preserving human freedom. Third, we must revitalize the concept of individual dignity and freedom by making democracy again a force that can capture the imagination and zeal of men everywhere.

When the problem is put in these general terms, the path of the free world might seem deceptively simple. Working out these principles in practice, however, will be a task that will challenge the greatest ingenuity of the political leadership of the future.

The Issue of Asia

The Western world has been slow to realize that Asia is in the grip of a deep-seated revolution the effects of which can make major alterations in the pattern of world politics. Keenly nationalistic, driven by an obsessive anti-colonialism and a nagging insistence on equality in status, the states of Asia are forcing themselves upon the attention of the Western world.

Great and small states alike are more significant in world affairs than they were a generation ago.

The world has yet to discover a basis for dealing effectively with this new feature of world affairs; many different approaches have been attempted, but none has had any real success.

The world can attain real stability only after these new participants in world politics have found their place in the pattern; as a result, the issue of Asia has become one of the critical problems of the future of world politics. Will Asia Become Communist? To many American the principal ground for concern about the 'new' Asia is that it is tending toward communism. Several Asian states—most notably China—have come under communist rule, and other states are in danger of slipping into the same orbit.

Yet we must not forget that communism did not make the Asian revolution; it has merely capitalized on it. Whether or not Asia becomes completely communist will in the last analysis depend not on what the communist do but rather on the policy of the West.

Asians are demanding internal and international freedom today; communism promises these and thus gains Asian loyalty. We in the West know the falsity of such communist gestures, but so far we have been unable to make either our rebuttals or our alternative proposals adequately palatable to Asians, whose fear of a renewed imperialism is almost pathological.

To save Asia from communism will require that we reformulate our appeals to Orientals—to take account of what they themselves want rather than what we should prefer that they have—and to back the appeals with action that is meaningful in Asian terms. Only in that way can the communist threat to Asia be stopped and perhaps turned back.

Can Asia Be Stabilized? Even if the communist danger to Asia be warded off, there remains a host of other problems. The most generalized of these is that of a chronic instability, international and domestic which affects almost the entire continent. So long as internal political convulsions and violent international controversies rack Asia, the world cannot know real peace.

Although any capsule solution to as huge and many-sided a problem as stability in Asia cannot help but be oversimplified, one general remark seems in point.

Asia's troubles stem generally from political immaturity: a driving energy is linked to a lack of experienced political leadership. Perhaps the west can make its greatest contribution to Asian stability by expediting the continent's orderly transition into maturity by giving assistance when it is asked for, exercising patience and tact, and always avoiding the appearance of seeking to impose intellectual or cultural domination. It may be that this will prove insufficient; perhaps.

Asia must suffer all the 'growing pains' which any adolescent passes through while becoming an adult. This would be unfortunate, but the West cannot count on stability in Asia until maturity comes to its young states.

The Issue of Atomic Energy

Much has been made of the importance of technology in contemporary world affairs. For most of us the problem is phrased most poignantly in terms of the issue of atomic energy. In this powerful force man has discovered a potentially revolutionary source of energy that could transform society, yet he is gripped by fear that this power will instead be used to destroy him.

Many observers feel that the final verdict on man's future on the earth will be rendered in terms of his ability to control the destructive implications of atomic energy and to release its potentiality for good.

Certainly none would deny that the next era of world history will be materially affected by the decisions arrived at concerning atomic power.

Can We Control the Bomb? Most urgent of the necessities facing the world in dealing with atomic energy is that of controlling its use as a weapon. If we cannot control it and if we are destined to be blown up by it the hopeful potential of atomic power turn out to be hollow mockery.

Devising a system for eliminating atomic weapons (for 'control' really means elimination) has so far proved impossible for statesmen, and the world has instead launched on an atomic-armaments race. No one is satisfied with this development, yet no acceptable alternative has yet been presented.

The attempts at control have failed up to now because of one major consideration; the large states have continued to feel that they would gain more from unilateral exploitation of atomic weapons than from any proposed control system that was mutually acceptable.

For real control to come about, all ration is worth more than any possible advantage to be gained from using the team only by a deliberate programme of voluntary self-restraint. So long as this attitude is not present and formalized, no control system can be really effective.

When and if the attitude does become general, the establishment of a control system will no longer be difficult. In this case, as in so many others, the final decision will be rendered not in the councils of statesmen but by the crystallization of public opinion around a particular point of view. Only the future can tell whether such opinion will form in time.

How Significant Are Atomic Weapons? In recent months a new dilemma has forced itself upon the attention of Americans. Conditioned since Hiroshima to the idea that atomic weapons are the decision-forcing tools of modern warfare, we have tended to place most, if not all, of our policy eggs in the atomic basket.

This idea became verbalized during 1954 and 1955 as the theory of 'massive retaliation.' The realization has slowly dawned, however, the Soviet possession of equally devastating weapons serves to neutralize whatever advantage we once might have had in atomic power. Mutual destruction is now possible.

This fact produces the disconcerting awareness that the true measure of military strength today is not really a nation's atomic capacity but rather its ability to wage 'conventional' war. Despite the formidable power represented by the bomb, the consequences of retaliation are so frightening that there is a strong possibility that atomic techniques will never again be used in war on a mass scale.

This throws us back to pre-atomic days in our calculations; the limited war discussed earlier as the only type man could afford will have to be waged with conventional weapons supplemented by 'tactical' atomic weapons, such as artillery.

Thus, the military aspect of atomic energy may well prove ultimately to be a monumental waste of time and resources; its principal result may be lingering resentments on the part of states who felt they were bullied and threatened by the states that possessed atomic weapons. This latter development is already partly realized.

Can We Realize the Atomic Potential? The other side of the coin of atomic energy is, of course, its peaceful exploitation. If control on its destructive power should be erected on an international basis, it would seem that they might constitute a framework for co-operation in making the advantages of atomic power available to the maximum number of people.

Such, at least was the import of President Eisenhower's atomic proposals to the United Nations in 1953; the first concrete steps toward the creation of a peaceful 'atomic pool' were taken during the summer of 1954.

The problem of harnessing this great force for human good is a technical one which we already know how to attack; political considerations alone stand in the way.

Here, too, we may remind ourselves that public opinion alone can decide whether we and our posterity are to enjoy the maximum advantages of this greatest of technological advances. In atomic power we have a tool of great possible value in attacking many of man's most deep-rooted problems. Only the mass of mankind can decide how soon and in what way the programme will be initiated.

The Issue of International Organization

One of the few relative certainties in the future of international politics is that there will be some form of international organization as long as the nation-state system holds together. We have ample evidence that the need for some such agency is so strongly felt and generally share that no one can conceive of doing without it.

The issue of international organization, therefore, is not really one of whether or not there shall be any, but is rather one of direction, form and degree.

It is a question of whether the international organization of the future will continue to be an adjunct process, co-existing with other methods of conducting international affairs, or whether it shall grow in importance until it eventually comes to occupy the keystone position in international society.

We have already considered these various alternatives. The problem is restated here so that at the end of our introduction to the study of international politics we may be reminded of one fundamental fact that bears upon the whole subject: institutions are vehicles of human action.

If we choose to follow a course that demands the elaboration and perfecting of the mechanisms of international organization, there can be no doubt that immediate improvement in the present procedures will take place.

If, on the other hand, we do not demand such extensive action requiring major institutional change, we may count upon a perpetuation of the present limited role of international organization.

The resolution of the issue of international organization, therefore, rests ultimately upon basic decisions yet to be made by man. If, for example, the decision of humanity is against war and the system that makes it possible, international organization may grow into a real instrument for world government.

If we decide, however, that these goals would require more of a sacrifice than we are prepared to make, international organization will remain of minor importance. No one can now predict which may humanity will decide.

Bibliography

Angell, Sir Norman, *The Great Illusion*, New York and London, Putnam, 1913.

Baldwin, Hanson, *The Price of Power*, New York, Harper, 1948.

Blanshard, Paul, *Democracy and Empire in the Caribbean*, New York, Macmillan, 1947.

Brown, Philip W., *International Society*, New York, Macmillan, 1923.

Burnham, James, *The Struggle for the World*, New York, John Day, 1947.

Bush, Vannevar, *Modern Arms and Free Men*, New York, Simon and Schuster, 1949.

Carr, Edward H, *The Twenty Years' Crisis, 1919-1939*, London, Macmillan, 1940.

Cassirer, Ernst., *The Myth of the State*, New Haven, Yale University Press, 1946.

Chase, E.P., *The United Nations in Action*, New York, McGraw-Hill, 1950.

Churchill, Sir Winston, *The Second World War*, 6 Vols., Boston, Houghton Mifflin, 1948-53.

Coker, Francis M, *Organismic Theories of the State*, New York, Columbia University Press, 1910.

Corbett, Percy, *Post-War Worlds*, Los Angeles, Institute of Pacific Relations, 1942.

Dahl, Robert A., *Congress and Foreign Policy*, New York, Harcourt Brace, 1950.

Davis, Elmer, *Two Minutes Till Midnight*, Indianapolis, Bobbs-Merrill, 1955.

Dennett, Raymond, and Johnson, Joseph (eds.), *Negotiating with the Russians*, Boston, World Peace Foundation, 1951.

Dulles, John Foster, *War or Peace?* New York, Macmillan, 1950.

Dulles, John Foster, *War or Peace?* New York, Macmillan, 1950.

Eagleton, Clyde, *Analysis of the Problem of War*, New York, Ronald, 1937.

Elliott, William Y., et al., *United States Foreign Policy, Its Organization and Control*, New York, Columbia University Press, 1952.

Fay, Sidney B., *The Origins of the World War*, 2nd, ed., New York, Macmillan, 1935.

Feller, Abraham, *The United Nations and World Community*, Boston, Little Brown, 1952.

Friedrich, Carl J., *Foreign Policy in the Making*, New York, Norton, 1938.

Halle, Louis J., *Civilization and Foreign Policy*, New York, Harper, 1955.

Haviland, H. Field, *The Political Role of the General Assembly*, New York, Carnegie Endowment, 1951.

Heilperin, Michael, *The Trade of Nations*, New York, Knopf, 1947.

Hemleben, S.J., *Plans for World Peace Through Six Centuries*, Chicago, University of Chicago Press, 1943.

Holcombe, Arthur, *Human Rights in the Modern World*, New York, New York University Press, 1948.

Hutchins, Robert A., et al., *Preliminary Draft of a World Constitu-*

tion, Chicago, University of Chicago Press, 1947.

Kahin, George Mc T., *Nationalism and Revolution in Indonesia*, Ithaca, Cornell University Press, 1952.

Keeton, George, *National Sovereignty and International Order*, London, Peace Book Company, 1939.

Kulischer, Eugene, *Europe on the Move*, New York, Columbia University Press, 1948.

Lauterpacht, Hersch, *The Function of Law in the International Community*, Oxford, Clarendon Press, 1933.

Leites, Nathan, *The Operation Code of the Politburo*, New York, McGraw-Hill, 1951.

Lie, Trygvie, *In the Cause of Peace*, New York, Macmillan, 1954.

Linton, Ralph (ed.), *Most of the World*, New York, Columbia University Press, 1949.

Lippmann, Walter, *The Cold War*, New York, Harper, 1947.

Maclaurin, John, *The United Nations and Power Politics*, New York, Harper, 1951.

McCamy, James D., *The Administration of American Foreign Affairs*, New York, Knopf, 1945.

Merriam, Charles E., *Political Power: Its Composition and Incidence*, New York, Whittlesey, 1934.

Mikesell, Raymond F. *United States Economic Policy and International Relations*, New York, McGraw-Hill, 1952.

Nicolson, Harold, *The Congress of C-Vienna: A Study in Allied Unity*, 1812-1822, New York, Harcourt Brace, 1946.

Northrop, F.S.C. *The Meeting of East and West*, New York, Macmillan, 1946.

Nussbaum, Arthur, *A Concise History of the Law of Nations*, Re. Ed., New York, Macmillan, 1954.

Ogburn, William F. (ed.), *Technology and International Relations*, Chicago, University of Chicago Press, 1949.

Opie, Redvers, et al., *The Search for Peace Settlements*, Washington, Brookings Institution, 1952.

Oppenheimer, Franz, *The State*, Indianapolis, Bobbs-Merrill, 1914.

Ralston, J.H., *International Arbitration from Athens to Locarno*, Stanford, Stanford University Press, 1929.

Ropke, Wilhelm, *The Solution to the German Problem*, New York, Putnam, 1946.

Russell, Bertrand, *Power: A New Social Analysis*, New York, Norton, 1938.

Schapiro, J. Salwyn, *The World in Crisis*, New York, McGraw-Hill, 1950.

Schuman, Frederick L., *Europe on the Eve: The Crisis of Diplomacy*, 1933-1939, New York, Knopf, 1939.

Schuman, Frederick L., *The Commonwealth of Man*, New York, Knopf, 1952.

Schuman, Frederick L., *The Commonwealth of Man*, New York, Knopf, 1952.

Soltau, Roger H., *An Introduction to Politics*, London, Longmans Green, 1951.

Somerville, John, *The Philosophy of Peace*, New York, Gaer Associates, 1948.

Strausz-Hupe, Robert, *The Balance of Tomorrow*, New York, Putnam, 1945.

Vagts, Alfred, *A History of Militarism*, New York, Norton, 1937.

Vogt, William, *Road to Survival*, New York, Sloane, 1948.

Walters, Frank P., *A History of the League of Nations*, London, Oxford University Press, 1952.

Warburg, James P., *How To Coexist Without Playing the Kremlin's Game*, Boston, Beacon Press, 1952.

White, Llewellyn, and Leigh, Robert D., *Peoples Speaking to Peoples*, Chicago, University of Chicago Press, 1946.

White, Theodore H., *Fire in the Ashes*, New York, Sloane, 1953.

Whyte, L.L., *Everyman Looks Forward*, New York, Henry Holt, 1948.

Wilcox, Clair, *A Charter for World Trade*, New York, Macmillan, 1949.

Wolfers, Arnold, *Britain and France Between Two Wars*, New York, Harcourt Brace, 1940.

Woodward, F.L., et al., *Foundations for World Order*, Denver, University of Denver Press, 1950.

Index

❑❑❑